Marvelous Reflections

By
Cecelia Frances Page

iUniverse, Inc.
New York   Bloomington

Marvelous Reflections

iUniverse books may be ordered through booksellers or by contacting:

iUniverse
1663 Liberty Drive
Bloomington, IN 47403
www.iuniverse.com
1-800-Authors (1-800-288-4677)

Because of the dynamic nature of the Internet, any Web addresses or links contained in this book may have changed since publication and may no longer be valid.

ISBN: 978-1-4502-0687-7 (sc)
ISBN: 978-1-4502-0688-4 (ebk)

Printed in the United States of America

iUniverse rev. date: 02/25/2010

CONTENTS

PREFACE

MARVELOUS REFLECTIONS is an exciting, stimulating book of 75 short stories and articles. This interesting book is about adventure topics, scientific issues, human interest stories, political issues, philosophical issues, nature topics and more.

SCIENTIFIC topics are Useful Inventions, Magnetism, Ocean Currents, Phenomenal Results, Organs In The Body, Solid Objects, Liquids and Gases, Use of Batteries and Extinction of Dinosaurs.

HUMAN INTEREST topics are Faith and Hope, Charities, Compatibility In Marriage, Losing Your Memory, The Secret Place, The Glass Menagerie, Uncertainties, The Pearl Necklace, Imagine If..., Being Admired and Appreciated, Personal Feelings, The Missing Link, Our Favorite Restaurants, A True Story About My Mother, About Audrey Hepburn, Party At The Beach, My Favorite Movies, Why Actors and Actresses Succeed, The Air Balloon, The Vacation, Living On A Raft, Middle Age Challenges, The Oldest Person, My Best Friend, Making Excuses, Memories, Around and Around We Go and Wanting Things.

NATURE topics are Water Lilies and Lotus Flowers, Caged Birds, Aquariums, Desert Experiences, Farmers Market, Moths, Butterflies and Fireflies and Marvels. PHILOSOPHICAL topics are Faith and Hope, Godly Deeds, Death and Rebirth, Memorable Awareness, Victories and Defeats, Attachment To Results, Middle Age Challenges, Beauty and Truth, Missionary Service and Brotherhood and Sisterhood.

POLITICAL ISSUES are Women's Rights, Taking Action, The White House in Washington D.C. and The Peace Corps Yesterday and Today. OTHER TOPICS are Rare Books, Playing String Instruments, Monitoring, Numbers, Big Cities, Mathematics In Daily Life, Spelling Correctly, The County Fair, Wood Carvings, Listening to Music, Timely Events, Paper Dolls, The Ballet, Interesting Times, Underwater Cities, The Time Machine, Beginnings and Endings, Random Occurrences and Explorations and Settlements.

ABOUT THE AUTHOR

Cecelia Frances Page began writing at age 19. Cecelia received a B.A. and M.A. in Education. She focused in Speech, English, Drama, Music and Psychology. Cecelia has written 50 books. She published 8 books on her own. 42 books were published by iUniverse, Incorporated. Cecelia is an author, educator, philosopher, musician, drama director, artist, photographer and voice and piano teacher. She is a vocal soloist as well. Cecelia Frances Page continues to write worthwhile books to inspire her readers.

Cecelia Frances Page has published five, original screenplays and three, original, poetry books. The original screenplays are entitled WALKING IN THE LIGHT, FLASHBACKS, CELESTIAL CONNECTIONS I and II and ADVENTURES IN LEMURIA. I and II. The three, original poetry books are entitled COSMIC DIMENSIONS, VIVID IMPRESSIONS and SIGNIFICANT INTROSPECTIONS. Cecelia Frances Page has written over five hundred, original poems. Several other poems are published in THE WORLD'S BEST POEMS OF 2004 and 2005.

Cecelia Frances Page's books published by iUniverse, Incorporation are entitled: WESTWARD PURSUIT, OPPORTUNE TIMES, IMAGINE IF…., FORTUNATELY, MYSTICAL REALITIES, MAGNIFICENT CELESTIAL JOURNEYS, EXTRAORDINARY ENCOUNTERS, BRILLIANT CANDOR, EXPAND YOUR AWARENESS, SEEK ENLIGHTENMENT WITHIN, VIVID MEMORIES OF HALCYON, AWAKEN TO SPIRITUAL ILLUMINATION, ADVENTURES ON ANCIENT CONTINENTS, PATHWAYS TO SPIRITUAL REALIZATON,

CELESTIAL CONNECTIONS, PHENOMINAL EXPERIENCES, CELESTIAL BEINGS FROM OUTER SPACE, AWESOME EPISODES, INCREDIBLE TIMES, INTERPRETATIONS OF LIFE, NEW PERSPECTIVES, TREMENDOUS MOMENTS, AMAZING STORIES AND ARTICLES, HORIZONS BEYOND, FASCINATING TOPICS, CERTAIN PEOPLE MAKE A DIFFERENCE, ADVENTUROUS EXPERIENCES, THE FUTURE AGE BEYOND THE NEW AGE MOVEMENT, POWER OF CREATIVE AND WORTHWHILE LIVING, EXTRATERRESTRIAL CIVILIZATIONS ON EARTH, RELEVANT INTERESTS, REMARKABLE WORLD TRAVELS, IMPRESSIONABLE OCCURRENCES, INFIINITE OPPORTUNITIES, RANDOM SELECTIONS, SIGNIFICANT MOMENTS, MARVELOUS REFLECTIONS, IMMENSE POSSIBILITIES and more.

Nonfiction

ONE
USEFUL INVENTIONS

Great inventors have changed cultures and they have produced worthwhile inventions that are very useful.

Jean Loucult, a French physicist, invented a pendulum in 1851 to prove for the first time in a laboratory that Earth rotates counterclockwise. A Loucult pendulum swings as the Earth turns beneath it. At the National Museum of American History in Washington D.C., this 240 pound, gold-plated, hollow bath hangs on a cable and topples pegs in a seemingly clockwise rotation that is an illusion.

Discoverers were darers who rode the oceans, climbed the mountains, and peered into the heavens. Inventors, in sharp contrast, were commonly artisans. Their habitat was the stuffy workshop where they forged axles, cut cogs on wheels and polished lenses and mirrors.

The brilliant, English philosopher-mathematician, William Whowell (1794-1866), said "described a cultivator of science in general." About the same time the realm of the artisan was being transformed and the word artist came into use to describe "one who practices a manual art in which there is much room for display of tastes; one who makes his craft a fine art."

"Leonardo was mentally a seeker after truth---a scientist; Correggio was an assertor of truth---an artist." Leonard Di Vinci was an inventor of various creations. He was an artist. Benjamin Franklin discovered the electrical kite and lightning rod. In a single, dangerous experiment he identified a new force. At once he provided a new device for the protection, propulsion and illumination of mankind. Electrical power and the invention of the internal-combustion engine was invented.

Spears, bows and arrows, throwing sticks, needles made from bone, harpoons, stone hammers, paintbrushes, combs and percussion fire making are some early inventions that were useful from 600,000 to 10,000 B.C. Boats were invented over 15,000 years ago, and possibly earlier. Long before 7,500 B.C. irrigation was developed. By 4000-3000 B.C. sailing vessels in Egypt were very well built.

Egypt developed cosmetics. The use of metal nails was discovered in the Tijuanaco ruins in the Andes and dated over ten thousands years ago. Nails were allegedly rediscovered in Europe, the Middle East and Near East about 3500 B.C. The wheel was rediscovered by Middle Eastern cultures about 3200 B.C. Plows were in use by many cultures before the Great Flood and became popular again by 3500 B.C. Hemp rope was created by 2800 B.C. Egyptians allegedly invented the five-stringed harp. An Egyptian hand mirror was created by 3500-3000 B.C.

Toilets were used by 2350 B.C. Egyptian clay balls were created by 2000 B.C. Chariots were created by 2000 B.C. Slings were used from 1400-1200 B.C. Wooden spears were invented long before 1500 B.C. Glass bottles were in common use by 1500 B.C. after rediscovery. Several very ancient civilizations have been excavated in recent years to prove that many inventions are much older than previously credited and developed by lost civilizations. Most of the inventions in this account are rediscoveries.

Sugar refining began 1000 B.C. Aqueducts were used in Atlantis and South America before 11,000 B.C. and rediscovered in Europe by 690 B.C. Iron saws were used in Europe by 1800-700 B.C. The abacas was created by 450 B.C. Water clocks were invented by 300 B.C. Musical organs were created by 300 BC. Musical organs were created by 300 B.C. Glassblowing was rediscovered by 100 B.C. Chinese carpets were created by 500 B.C.

Paper was reinvented by the Chinese. Chinese papermaking process became very useful. Wheelbarrows were used in Europe by 200-300 A.D.

Domes were created 124-128 A.D. in Europe and the Near East and in some pre-ice age, lost civilizations. Woodblock printing was used by 740 A.D. Windmills were invented in Persia. The spinning wheel was created by 1090 A.D.

The magnifying glass was created by 1200 A.D. The world continued to change from 1300 to 1779. More inventions were created such as gun powder, screw threads, optical discoveries and new developments in navigations. From 1300 to 1366 A.D. more inventions were created such as the alarm clock, lace and hand cannons. By 1400 oil painting was created. Screens and triggers were invented.

Between 1431 through 1550 A.D. the printing press, mariner's astrolabe, concave lenses, close-eye needle, the triple wheel, lock pistol, the grenade, hand painted wallpaper, bottle cork and diving bell were invented. By 1560 to 1600 B.C. more inventions were invented such as the telescope, compound telescope, thermometor, screw-cutting lathe, knitting machine, Mercator projection map and dredger.

From 1610 to 1700 A.D. inventions were created such as the slide rule, the calculator, Merry-Go-Round, the umbrella, pendulum clock, vacuum pump, flintlock firing mechanism and submarine. From 1660 to 1700 A.D. such inventions were created such as the megaphone, pocket-watch, precision microscope, steam pump, the clarinet, champagne, universal joint and Swedish bank note.

From 1700 to 1750 A.D. there were inventions such as the piano, baby carriage, atmospheric steam engine, the Caisson construction, machine gun, smelting and coke, orrery and octant. By 1740 to 1760 A.D. more inventions were created such as centigrade temperature, marine chronometer, sextant, carbonated water, lightning rod, Sheffield silver, Harrison's fourth chronometer and carbonated, water apparatus.

By 1760 to 1780 A.D. more inventions were created which are the hair hygrometer, sandwiches, spinning jenny, false teeth, steam engine, Cunnat's steam carriage, water-powered spinning machine and Arkwright's "flyer" spinning machine. By 1780-1870 steam power and the industrial revolution took place. Steam trains were invented. Robert Stephenson's "Rocket" locomotive was created by 1829. Photography was invented

Other inventions between 1829 to 1900 are the coin operated telephone, the Morse Code, the Sewing Machine, the hydrodermic syringe, the stapler, anesthetics, photocopier and miner's safety lamp.

Between 1780 to 1870 more inventions were the Whitney's cotton gin, Hiram S. Maxim's water cooled machine gun, use of Morton's ether inhaler, the bicycle, reaping machines and interchangeable parts to manufacture large numbers of goods. Between 1780 to 1810, other inventions were the steel-rib pen, double-acting steam machine, power loom, bifocal eyeglasses, hot-air balloon, parachute descent, ambulance and French guillotine.

Between 1795 to 1810 more inventions were created such as lithography, vaccinations, hydraulic press, Volta's batteries, gas stove, railroad locomotive, "Catch-Me-Who-Can locomotive and gas street-lighting. Between 1810 to 1830 more inventions were created such as canned food, spectroscope, stethoscope, hydraulic jack, Miner' Safety lamp, tunneling machine, revolver, macadamized roads, machine-made pins, electric motor, Faraday's electric motor, McCormick's reaper, water turbine, differential gear and electric motor.

From 1830 to 1850 more inventions were created such as Wheatstone and Cooke telegraph, electric telegraph, photographic negative, lawn mowers, dynamo transformer, combine harvester, velocipede, postage stamp, Christmas card, Morse Code, saxophone, micrometer, arc lamp, nitroglycerine, pneumatic tire and assembled rifle. From 1850 to 1900 more inventions were International Submarine Telegraph Cable, safety latch, ophthalmoscope, kerosene, vacuum tube, Coyley's band glider, airship, modular building system, can opener, Bunsen burner, Aniline dyes, steel manufacture, Otto's internal combustion engine, the Bessemer process for making steel and the Accumulator battery.

From 1860 to 1870 more inventions were created such as color photographs, linoleum, pasteurization, milking machine, plastics, machine-made spiral drill bit, Parkesine hair slide, underground railroad, London Metropolitan Railway steam locomotive, antiseptic surgery, riveting machine, air brakes, dry-cell battery, detonator, dynamite, torpedo, barbed wire, reinforced concrete, air-powered dental drill, Leclanche cell and geysers. Between 1870 to 1940 the automobile was commercialized. Charles Lindbergh made a flight in 1927. Faster communications took place because of electricity and wireless communications. Bakelite hair dry was invented. Gillette blades were produced for shaving. Orville and Wilbur Wright made the first powered flight in 1903. The invention of office equipment such as typewriters changed the way people worked.

MARVELOUS REFLECTIONS

From 1870 to 1900 more inventions were created such as photographic dry plates, chewing gum, margarine, monorail, the typewriter, the Bell telephone, Edison's phonograph, gelignite, Hughes' first microphone, phonograph record player, incandescent electric lamp, paper bag machine and electric train. The electric iron, steam turbine, streetcar, gasoline engine, fountain pen, linotype, seismograph, stereophone, Coca-Cola, motion pictures, disc record player, motorcycle, safety bicycle, electric stove, electric kettle, electric heater, automatic pistol, diesel engine, X-ray inflatable car tire, cathode-ray tube, aspirin, magnetic sound recording, taxicab meter and Bersey electric tax.

From 1900 to 1940 more inventions were created such as sound movies, vacuum cleaner, jukebox, autochrome photography, Geiger counter, sound radio broadcasting, Hoover Suction sweeper, food mixer, airmail, 35mm camera, zipper, traffic light, heat-resistant glass, flying boat and tank. More inventions were the lie detector, black and white television, color television, insulin, antibiotics, bulldozer, submarine gun, highways, liquid-filled rocket, Whittle jet engine, automatic, whole garment, knitting machines, pop-up toaster, electron microscope, radar, nylon, polyethylene, DDT insecticide, helicopter, parking meter and stabilizers.

The changing world from 1940 to 2000 brought nuclear energy, computers, credit cards, the jet age, space travel, robots, genetic engineering, missiles, aerosol can, nuclear reactors, atomic bombs, transistors, microwave ovens, scuba diving, heart-lung machines, transistor radios, oral contraceptives, heart pacemakers, fiber-optic endoscopes, videotapes, integrated circuits, space satellites, atomic power stations and Hovercrafts. More inventions were the electric toothbrush, cassette tape recorder, word processor, skateboard, lasers, scanning electron microscope, satellite navigation, automatic landing, floppy disks, early home video games, CT scanner, food processors, Apple II personal computer, personal stereo, wave-powered generator, supersonic passenger service and catalytic Converters, satellite TV, Rubik's cube, artificial heart, genetic fingerprinting, gene gun, wind farming, Space Shuttle Columbia, video telephones, human genome map, micro engineering, smart card for telephone payment, zero-emission vehicle and genetic engineering of animals and plants. Voice recognition where one's thoughts are recorded with a voice to repeat your thoughts is one of the greatest inventions.

Hundreds of useful inventions have been created over a period of many years. Within the past 200 years more inventions have been created to help mankind to have more conveniences to create better living conditions.

After 2000 remote controlled, high flying jet planes were manufactured to video and search territory. Laser and ultrasound frequencies were used for surgery, healing, growing hair and eliminating body fat. Natural cures without dangerous side effects became available to treat all major diseases. Solar energy fields were productive. Hand-held, electronic encyclopedias were created. Internet downloads of movies and music videos were connected to television screens. High resolution, digital, flatscreen TV was popular. Hand-held internet and computer games were manufactured. Cell phones took photos and videos and incorporated email, texts and music downloads. Computer screened, detailed, color photos of both sides of all streets, highways, freeways and scenery in thousands of cities showed drivers how to find homes, businesses and recreational facilities. Laser holograms created people, animals and objects that looked real from a distance and moved, talked and behaved. Robot pets became popular in Japan. Home computers produced daily newspapers, weekly and monthly magazines and computer books. A twenty story, gigantic cruise ship was completed that had a golf course, botanical garden, amusement park, sports stadium, music concert pavilion, several restaurants, gym, spa, swimming pool, beauty parlor and luxuries of a five star hotel.

Nonfiction

TWO
MAGNETISM

Magnetism is defined by Webster's Dictionary as "the property, quality or condition of being magnetic. Magnetism is the force to which this is due. Magnetism is the branch of physics dealing with magnets and magnetic phenomena. Magnetism effects magnetoelectricity designating electricity produced by changing magnetic fields in the vicinity of electric conductors.

"Hydrodynamics is the science that deals with the interaction of a magnetic field with an electrically conducting liquid. A magnometer is an instrument for magnetically detecting concealed metallic weapons on the person.

Magnetism effects gravitational pull of the planets in our solar system. Gravity holds objects on the Earth. Electromagnetism effects how electricity is used on the Earth. Electric charges occur frequently in Nature. Humanity has learned to use electricity. Magnetic currents affect magnetic objects. Heavy stones can be moved by magnetism called levitation. Ancient Lemurians and Atlanteans knew how to use levitation to lift large objects.

Magnetism has existed for millions of years on Earth. Rocks have been moved from one place to another by natural forces. Continents have moved gradually because of gradual sliding and magnetic forces. Magnetism is necessary so that objects can move and change.

Electromagnetism is a natural force inside of the center of the Earth. Electromagnetic forces effect the movement of the Earth as it rotates and revolves around the Sun. The law of magnetism operates based on light, motion and attraction in Nature.

"The difference between mundane electricity and the magnetic energy of the human body is the difference between the covered and the uncovered spark or fiery life." according to the Temple Teachings in Volume One. It has been a mystery to investigators of electric phenomena as to just what constituted the difference between magnetism and electricity. Electricity cannot be generated without the use of a magnetic field. Electricity, being the spiritual force, must have a material medium in which to manifest, and the magnetic field is that medium.

The manasic centers of the brain are dependent on magnetism for life expression on the physical plane. Any concentrated effort of the physical substance which forms the outer wall of each molecule of that substance, to the individual Higher self. It is not so protected when the center is used by the lower self in defiance of the aforesaid evolutionary law. Fohatic energy creates magnetism.

Fiction

THREE
FAITH AND HOPE

Faith and hope are important attributes to acquire. Someone with faith believes in supporting a cause and purpose regarding a specific issue and problem. Faith is unquestionable belief that does not require proof or evidence. Faithful people have complete trust, confidence and self reliance.

People who have hope have desires accompanied by expectations. A person wants something very much. A person expects to receive what he or she wants.

Emmet Jamison, who lived in Portland, Oregon, had faith that God existed. Emmet was suffering from paralysis in his spine. He was unable to walk. He was strapped into a wheelchair during the day. He was put in a bed with sliding metal protective bars at night. Emmet had suffered from paralysis for ten years. He had been in an automobile accident which caused his handicapped condition.

Emmet prayed that he would be healed of the spinal paralysis which afflicted him for ten years. He prayed to God every day to heal him. Emmet had to adjust to his paralysis which caused him to become numb. He had to depend on his wife to take care of him. He invited his friends to come to his house to visit with him.

Emmet's friends sympathized with him about his handicapped situation. He used his hands to push buttons on his automatic wheelchair to control his wheelchair. He went out into the backyard of his home to sit in the sun. He liked to quiet his mind while he felt the cool breeze on his body. He sniffed the fragrance of the flowers, trees and shrubs in the backyard. Emmet enjoyed observing the flowers and trees blowing in the wind. He watched bees and butterflies moving about on the flowers and shrubs. His friends sat near Emmet in garden chairs. His friends observed Emmet enjoying the garden.

Emmet's friends admired him for being able to have faith in God. They knew Emmet prayed to God to overcome his spinal paralysis. His friends realized that Emmet had not given up about having a normal life.

Emmet was examined by a number of doctors who X-rayed his spine during his ten years of paralysis. Finally, Emmet was examined by a well known surgeon who had been able to do surgery on the spine. The doctor's name was Dr. Joshua Nelson, a specialist in bone and muscle surgery. Dr. Nelson took many X-rays of Emmet's spine and back muscles.

Dr. Joshua Nelson looked closely at the spine and muscle X-rays. He noticed why Emmet was experiencing paralysis. He wanted to perform surgery on Emmet to cure Emmet of the paralysis by adjusting his spine and cleaning excess blood in the back tissue. Dr. Nelson told Emmet that he might be able to relieve pinched nerves and build back muscles.

It was Emmet's decision to have constructive surgery. He felt it was worth having surgery. So, Emmet told Dr. Nelson that he would have exploratory surgery. The surgery was scheduled. Emmet was excited that Dr. Nelson was going to attempt to stop the spinal paralysis.

Three weeks later Emmet went to the hospital with his wife. He was prepared for surgery by several nurses. Emmet was taken to surgery. Dr. Joshua Nelson began surgery as soon as Emmet received enough anesthesia. He took surgical instruments to cut into Emmet's spine and muscle tissue. Dr. Nelson relieved Emmet's spine by adjusting several vertebras. Then he cleaned ruptured tissue and drained out muscle tissue. Dr. Nelson sewed up the incisions after finishing the surgery.

Nurses kept an eye on Emmet after surgery in the recovery room until he woke up. They kept warm blankets over him to keep him warm. When Emmet finally woke up he looked around the recovery room. He realized that the surgery was over. He hoped he would no longer be paralyzed. He wanted very much to walk again.

Dr. Nelson came by to talk to Emmet later that day about the surgery. Emmet had been rolled down to a room in Intensive Care in the hospital in Portland, Oregon. Dr. Nelson told Emmet that he had removed obstructions in his spine. A ruptured disc had been removed. Excess blood had been drained near the spine in the muscle tissue. Dr. Nelson was positive and hopeful. He told Emmet that he believed Emmet would recover. He also said he believed Emmet would be able to walk again after daily recovery and physical therapy.

Emmet was glad to hear what Dr. Nelson said about his ability to recover in time. Emmet's prayers had been answered. He had faith that God would help him recover. Now he had the opportunity to walk again so he could have a normal, active life again. Emmet continued to have faith and hope that he would recover soon. He went to physical therapy every day to strengthen his body muscles.

Gradually Emmet began to walk a little at a time. He started by holding onto side bars with his arms. He lifted one leg at a time in order to strengthen his leg muscles. He was no longer paralyzed because the obstruction in his spine had been removed. Day by day he became stronger. Finally, he was able to walk back and forth across the area where the metal bars were. Then, he began to walk with crutches. After a period of time he walked using a cane. Finally, he walked without a cane. Then he was able to walk normally again.

Emmet was able to drive a car again. He took daily walks down the street and back. He was able to go shopping and swimming. Emmet could enjoy eating out at restaurants. He even walked on the beach to exercise. He enjoyed sunsets while he was at the beach. Because of his faith and hope in resolving his problems he was able to recover and live a normal life again.

Nonfiction

FOUR
CHARITIES

Different, charitable organizations exist in the world. Charity organizations reach out to help impoverished people in underprivileged countries. CARE Incorporated, Peace Corps, UNESCO and many church charities exist. The Salvation Army is another helpful organization which serves the underprivileged and homeless people in America.

Local churches prepare free, hot meals every day for homeless, poverty-stricken people. They serve a variety of main dishes with vegetables and fruit as well as milk, tea and coffee. Christian women collect canned food to send to churches.

The Salvation Army provides inexpensive clothes, blankets, shoes and many other items for many people who have little money. A shirt may cost 50 cents. A blouse may cost 50 cents. A pair of pants may cost 75 cents. A pair of shoes may cost $1.00. These same people would have to pay a lot less money for these items. The Salvation Army provides shelters for the needy, homeless people. Shelters provide beds and some food in clean surroundings.

Charities have provided many needy people with basic needs. Charitable people are very helpful and generous by donating money, household goods and food. Many people are in need of food and shelter. They depend on others.

MARVELOUS REFLECTIONS

Sometimes charity balls and dinners are given in order to raise enough money to help needy causes and people. Charities are worthwhile because many needy people are benefited by charitable endeavors. So, contribute to charities to help needy people.

Nonfiction

FIVE
WOMENS RIGHTS

W omen have rights just like men. For many centuries many women have been extremely restricted, mistreated and abused. Men have dominated women for thousands of years. Women were not allowed to make major decisions or to vote. They were expected to remain submissive and obedient to men.

There have been some matriarchal societies throughout history. There was an Amazon civilization of women who lived in South America who lived near the Amazon River. Only women lived in this civilization. Men were allowed to visit occasionally for mating purposes. Women were treated equally in the Minoan civilization in the Mediterranean Sea. There were Minoan goddesses. They made many decisions. Ancient Sumerians treated women equally. Men revered and respected women.

Women in America and Australia have striven to be treated equally. Women are given the opportunity to vote. More women have become senators, representatives and mayors in America. Women have become leaders and politicians in the Western civilizations.

However, many women are still dominated by religious beliefs in the Middle East and Near East. Many women in Africa and parts of South America are not free to make major decisions. They still live by restricted, traditional beliefs and expectations. Women who are raped and beaten are being abused. They need to be given their freedom. They need the same opportunities women of the West have been given. Slavery of women takes place around the world.

Equality between men and women is important. Without equality it is difficult for women to be free to express their opinions and to live freely. Women are the mothers. Their sense of well being is important for the progress made in each civilization. Women, who are free, should fight for the rights of all women around the world.

Nonfiction

SIX
COMPATABILITY IN MARRIAGE

Compatibility is very important in marriage. To get along with your life mate helps a marriage to last. Couples who have things in common are able to share hobbies and interests. Sharing common interests helps to bring couples closer together.

Couples who communicate their feelings, opinions and beliefs effectively are able to voice their thoughts. The more a couple expresses their viewpoints the more they realize how they feel about their lives. Effective communications makes a difference in a relationship.

There are couples who have 50th anniversaries who state that they are still happy together. These couples have learned to communicate well. They have become closer and closer through the years. They have learned to become compatible by sharing their values, feelings and deeper thoughts. Many couples believe in God and Jesus Christ. They pray to God to strengthen their marriages.

During difficult times successful couples endure hardships. They manage to work out their problems. They may face economic strife. Infidelity may be another problem. Couples must learn to forgive their weaknesses and shortcomings. When personal problems occur they find solutions to solve their problems.

Compatibility is the key to a successful marriage. Learn to accept shortcomings and human errors. Forgive past wrongdoings in a relationship. Avoid speaking extremely harsh words to your spouse. Find ways to avoid arguing and fighting. Try to resolve problems peacefully. Try to maintain harmony and a positive attitude no matter what problems exist in your marriage. Try to maintain a compatible relationship with your mate.

Nonfiction

SEVEN
LOSING YOUR MEMORY

People tend to lose their memories as they get older. Why do they lose their memories? Older people accumulate toxins and misqualified energy in their bodies. This accumulation of negative substances may cause memory loss. A lack of certain hormones may cause dark substances to clog up nerve ends in the brain near the memory bank.

Eating a wide variety of organic fruits and vegetables as well as organic grains and nuts will keep the body healthy. Fresh food is important to eat. When the body is healthy the brain is healthier. The memory bank should function much better when a person is healthy.

Vigorous exercise stimulates the blood stream and nervous system. When the blood is normal and the nervous system is functioning well, the brain operates normally.

Certain foods such as canned foods, highly rich, greasy, fatty foods can eventually affect the memory bank in the brain. Old food, overcooked food and processed foods with chemicals in them are not healthy to eat.

Metal and aluminum pans are not healthy to use to cook in. Aluminum gets into the food causing loss of memory in the brain. This unnatural substance causes damage to the bran. People suffer from Alzheimer's disease and dementia because of the use of aluminum.

So, cook with stainless steel pots and pans which are safe without unsafe metals and aluminum. Avoid unnecessary heat on most foods. Preserve the life force in the food you eat.

Use your mind frequently to recall and remember ideas and knowledge. You should exercise your memory and stay alert and aware of your environment. Keep your mind stimulated to maintain your memory. You do not have to lose your memory.

Nonfiction

EIGHT
RARE BOOKS

Rare books are books which may be unavailable because there are very few in existence. Ancient Bibles are kept in museums in glass cases. Historians are studying ancient Bibles.

Original books are rare books. When a few books only exist for a given book these books are rare. The original book of ALICE IN WONDERLAND is the original, written version with original illustrations.

Shakespeare's original books of his Shakespearean plays are rare books. His original plays were written in his handwriting. It was years later that Shakespeare's plays were published.

Ralph Waldo Emerson's original books were published over one hundred years ago. A few older editions of his well known essays are rare today. THE PROPHET by Jagel Gibran was published nearly a century ago. There are few of these books on public library shelves and few of these books are in bookstores. This book is becoming rare.

Books that are no longer published become rare books because few of these books still exist. THE ATLANTIS CONSPIRACY by Dr. Maxine Asher is a rare book because only seven copies were in existence in 1975. Dr. Asher stated where Atlantis once existed and her diving expedition found the ruined city where Plato said it was located. It fell into the Atlantic Ocean off the coast of Spain.

MARVELOUS REFLECTIONS

ONE HUNDRED THOUSAND YEARS OF MANKIND'S UNKNOWN HISTORY was written by Robert Charroux. He described unusual historical events that have taken place throughout history in ancient civilizations such as in Sumeria, Babylonia, Europe, Egypt, South America and lost empires. This explorer and archaeologists researched many obscure and generally unknown ancient writings from around the world. Robert Charroux lived in France and relatively few copies of his six volumes are found in America today.

Another rare book is the ancient VYMANIKA SHAASTRA text, written in Vedic India, that clearly describes pilot training, flight paths, individual parts of flying machines, clothing for pilots and passengers and the food recommended for long flights. Included in these writings, which are over 5000 years old, is technical detail on the metals used and propulsion units.

BOOK OF DZYAN is from India and written over 3000 years ago describing ancient aircraft, spacecraft, advanced technology and nuclear war. This book is no longer in print. Only a few copies of this book exist today.

THE BOYS FROM TOPSIDE was written by Wilburt B. Smith in 1970 and is very rare and out of print. This volume is about Project Magnet, the Canadian government's former, top secret investigation of UFOs. This book includes an actual contact landing of a flying saucer and meeting with the occupants at a secret UFO contact station in Alberta, Canada. Technological information was provided.

MATRIX, in three volumes, was written by Val Valarian in the 1980s to 1990s. These huge books were the most detailed ever published concerning secret technology, underground bases and cities. The book detailed many secret contacts with alien civilizations and hundreds of conspiracies during the last 5000 years. The hidden truths of all major events, all types of metaphysics, secret societies, secret science, alien agendas, time travel, other dimensions, world economics, diseases, world organizations and hidden, alternative histories are detailed in this book. These books are over 1000 pages each. These volumes are not found in chain book stores and have not appeared in advertisements for many years. So, they are very rare.

Another rare book is THE BOOK OF INVASIONS. It is a very old volume from Ireland. Details of Atlantis and its destruction are described in this book. OERA LINDA gives details of the sinking of Atlantis about 11,500 years ago. This very old book is from Scandinavia. It was written in ancient times. It has become a rare book. CHILAM BALAM is a rare, ancient, Mayan text describing the destruction of lost continents that sank in the Atlantic and Pacific oceans. These have been interpreted by some researchers as Atlantis and Mu.

Nonfiction

NINE
WATER LILIES AND LOTUS FLOWERS

Water lilies are magnificent flowers that grow in water. Many water lilies grow in ponds in gardens and meadows. Water lilies are white with yellow centers. Their petals spread out when they emerge in ponds.

Water lilies have large, green leaves around them. They add to the ponds with their splendid beauty. Lilies are put in bouquets in vases. They stand out in the bouquet.

Lotus flowers grow in water. They grow in ponds and in large fountains. The lotus flower is also white with gold centers. Lotus flowers have unfolding, white petals. They look spectacular as they emerge in ponds with broadleaf leaves surrounding them.

Lilies and lotus flowers are considered to be spiritual flowers. Their petals represent their spiritual unfoldment. Lotus flowers have been worshipped for thousands of years in the Far East.

Nonfiction

TEN
PLAYING STRING INSTRUMENTS

There are a variety of string instruments that can be played. There are the violin, viola, cello, guitar, harp ukulele and zither. Each of these string instruments has a certain tone quality. Each string instrument is a different size. Therefore, the smaller the string instrument, it has a higher tone quality. The larger the string instrument the deeper and lower the tone quality. The Bass Viol has the deepest, lower tones.

The violin has strings. A bow, made of fine horse hair attached to a wooden backing, is used to move against the violin strings which are tightened wires attached to the violin. Each tone is created with the vibration of the bow strings moving firmly on the violin strings. Violin and viola strings must be tightened so notes are on pitch. The violin is made with a scroll, pegs, a neck, finger board, tailpieces and chinboard. A violin is held horizontally under the chin, resting against the collarbone.

The viola is slightly larger than a violin. The tones on a viola are more mellow and deeper and tuned a fifth lower. The cello is an instrument in the violin family between the viola and double bass string instrument in size and pitch. It is a much larger, string instrument. The cello is placed on the floor with a cello brace. The tones of the cello strings are much deeper and richer than a violin or viola. The strings on a cello are longer and thicker. The cello bow is much bigger. Cello tones are more powerful.

The bass viol is much bigger than the cello. It is the largest of the string instruments. The bass viol is placed on the floor on a bass viol brace. The bass viol bow is much larger than other string instrument bows. The deepest and richest lower tones are played on the bass viol.

All string instruments, such as the violin, viola, cello and bass viol family, are played with bows and one's finger. Strings can be plucked as well. Plucking sounds are more emphasized when played.

The guitar is played only with fingers played on guitar strings. Guitar players pluck the strings of a guitar carefully to play tunes. Some guitar players play by ear. They can stand or sit in a chair while playing the guitar. Most guitars have six strings. Some guitars have twelve strings. A guitar pick is used to produce special, staccato sounds on guitars.

Zithers look different than other string instruments. A zither is made in a rectangular shape with pointed corners. The strings are spread out. A zither is a musical instrument having from thirty to forty strings stretched across a flat soundboard and played with a spectrum and fingers.

Each of the string instruments are played as solo instruments in the orchestra. Banjos are round, smaller instruments. The strings have an in between sound and country music is played with banjos and guitars.

Fiction

ELEVEN
THE SECRET PLACE

Secret places are where we can experience privacy, solitude and to retreat to rest, hide and remove ourselves from others. Secret places may be in a private, secret room in our home. Secret caves where we can hide and retreat in may be available. A private, remote beach may be another secret place. Whenever we can get away from people and crowds in isolated places, other people do not know about, may help us retreat from the busy, "hum drum" of life.

Judy Hendricks lived in Chicago, Illinois where there are many people. Certain streets are very crowded with many cars driving by and many people walking down the streets. The sound of cars and car horns, ambulance and police car sirens echo in the city of Chicago.

Judy wanted to retreat to a secret place away from the busy confusion in her daily life in the city. So, she decided to find a secret place to get away from the noise and crowded conditions. She lived in an apartment on the sixth floor in a big, apartment complex. She could hear many sounds in the apartment complex such as loud radios and stereos, crying babies, vacuum cleaners, loud talking and city sounds nearby. Judy was tired of hearing these distractive sounds. She wanted to feel peace and harmony in a quiet place.

MARVELOUS REFLECTIONS

Judy decided to pack her luggage and drive her car out of the busy city of Chicago to some secluded place far away. Once her belongings for her journey were packed and placed in her two door sedan, she drove out of the city onto a freeway towards the East Coast to the Atlantic Ocean. As she traveled east she saw different places where there were meadows, forests and mountains. She passed several lakes.

One lake was quite large with deep, blue water. Judy stopped to wade in the cool water. She observed geese, ducks, mud hens and blackbirds hovering in the lake and near this scenic lake. Few people were around. She didn't consider this to be a secret place however. She got back in her car and continued driving east. It took her at least 16 hours to reach the East Coast.

The Atlantic Ocean was a deep, blue color. Judy had arrived at a pristine beach along the coast of North Carolina. She was glad to breathe the fresh air and to feel cool breezes. It was early spring. Judy walked on the long, wide, white sand beach. She enjoyed going barefooted on the smooth sand. She heard seagulls squawking as they flew over her head and landed on the beach. She watched the seagulls as they flocked together.

Judy kept walking on the beach until she came to some hidden caves which were inside a large cliff. Judy decided to explore these hidden caves. She walked past an ocean tide pool. She saw sea-urchins, clams, mussels and starfish in the tide pool as she walked by. She was fascinated when she observed the sea life on the tide pool. Judy continued on until she reached the entrance of one of the caves.

As Judy walked deeper and deeper into the dark cave she saw mussels and barnacles clinging on rocks and on the wall of the cave. She saw more smaller, rock pools with small fish swimming in them. Judy carefully studied these pools with the small fish in them.

Judy came to the back of the big cave. She decided to sit down on a cluster of rocks to rest. She felt she had found her secret place at last. Judy rested on the big rock. She was glad to find a quiet, remote place. She didn't hear city noises and human sounds pounding in her ears. She felt relaxed and at peace. She heard the splashing waves and currents of the ocean. The rhythm of the ocean was soothing.

The big, remote cave was an ideal place to get away from the "hum drum" of everyday life in the city. Judy stayed in this cave for several hours. It began to get dark outside. The sun was going over the horizon. Judy did not have a flashlight. The big cave was becoming very dark.

Judy realized that she would have to leave this dark cave before it became completely dark outside. Judy struggled to find her way out of the cave. She bumped into rocks. The ocean waves were splashing into this cave. Judy became wet all over from the rising water. Judy was shivering from the splashing waves. She was worried she would be trapped in this cave because the ocean waves kept rising higher. She finally had to swim against the crashing, cold water in order to get out of the cave.

Judy finally swam out of the cave. The big, tide pool was covered with ocean water. Judy was forced to swim against the ocean currents because the ocean water had risen at least 10 to 12 feet. Judy was only 5 feet 3 inches in height. Judy kept swimming in the ocean until she came to the edge of the beach. She was no longer in the ocean.

Judy was exhausted because of her struggle to reach the higher ledge away from the rising, ocean water. Judy rested on the ledge. She was shivering because she was soaking wet. Judy got up and walked over to her car. She changed her clothes after drying her body from the cold, ocean water. She put on a warmer jacket. She put on shoes once her feet were dry.

Judy got into her car. She rested in the front seat in the drivers' seat. She was relieved to be in her car. The secret place in the cave was not a safe place to dwell for many hours because the ocean waves came into the cave and flooded the cave for many hours. Judy realized that she could find peace and harmony within herself once she looked within to maintain a tranquil state of consciousness. She could reach a secret place within her higher consciousness.

Fiction

TWELVE
THE GLASS MENAGERIE

A variety of glass objects were on a shelf in the home of Juhl and Jared Thomas. Juhl had gathered these glass blown objects. Juhl and Jared looked closely at glass blown horses, seahorses, cats, zebras and flowers. These glass blown objects were exciting to look at.

Juhl and Jared had made a hobby of gathering glass blown objects from glass factories. Some of their glass menagerie were purchased in Venice in Italy. The colors reflected in the glass objects gleamed when sunlight beamed through the windows. Juhl and Jared enjoyed observing changing colors reflected in each glass blown object.

Juhl moved the glass objects around so the light would continue to gleam through the objects. She had become attached to her glass menagerie. She dusted each glass object carefully at least once a week. Juhl and Jared had spent a lot of money for these glass objects. Juhl and Jared didn't want anything to happen to their glass menagerie.

When the Thomas's went anywhere they locked their house. They didn't want anyone to rob them of their glass menagerie display. Several years went by and the glass menagerie became larger and larger. Juhl and Jared took care of their glass collection.

Then, one day there was a severe earthquake. The collection of glass objects fell off the shelf onto the hard floor. All of them broke except one glass horse. Juhl and Jared came home that night from their jobs. They noticed the broken, glass objects on the floor. They were heart broken when they saw the shattered glass objects.

Juhl picked up the one, unbroken glass horse. She wondered why it didn't break like the other shattered objects. She wiped this object carefully. Then she placed it back on the shelf. The shelf looked empty and colorless. Juhl felt very sad and despondent. She missed her collection of glass objects. She would have to collect a new collection of glass objects in order to have another display of many glass blown objects. It would cost more money.

Juhl decided to select more glass objects to begin a new collection of colorful, gleaming objects to look at. Juhl was willing to spend more money to buy her new collection. Jared spent money on the new, glass collection. She hoped there would never be another, severe earthquake. She created a large, wall riming around the shelf so the new, glass menagerie was collected. Juhl and Jared felt their new, glass collection would be safe.

Fiction

THIRTEEN
UNCERTAINTIES

Many uncertainties occur around us and to us. We are uncertain about when severe earthquakes and floods will take place. We are uncertain about tsunamis destroying many places on Earth. We are uncertain about global warming and its effect on Earth. We are uncertain about when we will die.

Many people are uncertain about reincarnation. Many people still believe we have only one life. People do not believe we have many embodiments. They are uncertain about living many lives.

Uncertainties cause people to have doubts, fears and questions about things they do not understand. People are uncertain about what will happen on Earth day by day, month by month and year by year.

How can we deal with uncertainties? We need to be objective in order to seek truth and knowledge in order to understand what is occurring and happening around us. Uncertainties are caused because of ignorance and unexpected cause and effect situations. We need to overcome fear of uncertainties by learning the cause and effect behind every uncertain occurrence.

William Sampson lived near the ocean in Washington State. He was very inquisitive. He asked a lot of questions about unknown topics and situations. William wanted to learn what caused tsunamis. He found out why large tidal waves occur during a tsunami. He found out what causes severe earthquakes. He began to understand why seasons were formed.

William found that tsunamis were caused by severe earthquakes and large landslides which cause enormous, tidal waves. Very large tidal waves sweep over many miles of land destroying everything because of severe flooding.

William learned that the distance of the Sun to Earth effects changing climates. He found out that colder climates occur in the Northern Hemisphere as a rule.

William wondered about UFOs appearing in the sky over different locations. He wondered where they were coming from. He hoped UFOs would not cause destruction on the Earth. So he studied about them by doing research in the public libraries and bookstores. He read about other peoples' experiences with UFOs. He found out that extraterrestrials have been visiting the Earth for thousands of years. Many people have been abducted by aliens. They have been experimented on. Interbreeding has occurred with aliens to produce hybrids of new human beings on Earth.

William felt uncertain about UFOs and alien beings coming to Earth. He didn't want to be abducted by them. He saw videos and films about UFOs and aliens coming from outer space to Earth. He tried to overcome his fear of them. He hoped aliens were coming in peace with a purposeful mission to help humanity on Earth.

William attempted to resolve all his uncertainties so that he would not have too many doubts as well as experiencing unnecessary fears and anxieties about the unknown.

Nonfiction

FOURTEEN
MONITORING

Monitors help keep order, records and attendance. A person monitors a foreign broadcast. Monitoring is any of various devices for checking and regulating the performance of machines, aircraft, guided missiles, etc. Monitoring is to test for radioactive contamination with a monitor. Monitoring is used to listen in on a foreign broadcast, telephone conversation, etc. as well as gathering political or military information. Monitoring is to check the quality of transmission with a monitor.

It is important to keep an accurate attendance in school. Teachers and school officer personnel need to keep records of the attendance if certain students are frequently absent. Truant officers need to use school attendance records to prove who are not attending school regularly. Absentees are investigated so they are warned about missing too much school. They must attend school regularly.

Teachers keep classroom records of attendance and grades for each subject. Students receive report cards during each school year. Report cards are records. All grades are recorded in each student's school file. Records are kept for each student from kindergarten all the way through high school. Records of school progress need to be kept in order for teachers to evaluate students' progress. Teachers keep a complete, written record of each student's attendance, accomplishments and grades. Recorded information is used to check student strengths and weaknesses.

Machines, aircraft and missiles are carefully monitored. They are carefully checked and records are kept about the parts in these devices. It is important to check and label each part in a machine, aircraft and missile. Specific parts can be identified readily. Store catalogs in Sears and motor shops have pictures of machine parts. Machine factories use catalogs to look up missile and aircraft parts so they can order new parts needed to build as well as to repair specific machines, aircraft and missiles. Monitoring is an important way to keep track of valuable records, parts listings and specific information.

Nonfiction

FIFTEEN
NUMBERS

Numbers are symbols to measure amounts. Numbers have been created many thousands of years ago. There are even numbers and odd numbers. Even numbers are 2, 4, 6, 8, 10, 12, 14, 16, 18, 20, etc. Odd numbers are 1, 3, 5, 7, 9, 11, 13, 15, 17, 19, etc. There are prime numbers which do not factorize. Examples 2, 3, 5, 7, 11, 13, 17, 19, 23, 29, 31, 37, 41, 43, 47... Note that 4= 2x2, 6= 2x3, 9= 3x3; so they are not prime numbers.

Question: Find the lowest 10 numbers which are not primes and the next five numbers greater than 47 which are prime numbers.

Numbers are quantities as consisting of units. Numbers designate how many. Numbers of dollars and cents indicate the value of money used such as pennies, nickels, dimes, one dollar bills, ten dollar bills, twenty dollar bills, one hundred dollars and thousands dollars, etc.

Question: Write the following sums of money in dollars and cents: a)   1 dollar and 5 cents = $1.05, b) 2 dollars and 50 cents, c) 5 dollars and 27 cents, d) 27 dollars and 25 cents e) Write 5 more sums of money each greater than 27 dollars and 25 cents.

f) Add the following sums of money: c = $4.25 + $1.05 + $3.20 + $7.35

Without numbers as symbols for amounts it would be difficult to communicate how many things exist. When things are subtracted things are taken away. We need to be able to count objects, people, money and many other things. Numbers began before counting existed. Numbers are used in the field of mathematics. There are single numbers and groups of 2 place, 3 place, 4 place and 5 place numbers, etc.

Numbers are added in small groups and larger groups. Numbers are even used in word problems. We learn to count from 0 to 500 in Grades 1, 2 and 3. Then we learn place value as we count by tens, hundreds, thousands, millions, billions, trillions and zillions. We learn place value so we can add, subtract, multiply and divide correctly.

Numbers are recorded in ledgers, in bookkeeping books, in tablets, in banks, on computers and in math books. We use numbers in calendars. Numbers and symbols are used in algebra, geometry, calculus, trigonometry as well as general math. We will continue to use numbers.

Mathematics includes Algebra, which is used for solving problems using x is the number we are trying to find. Several problems follow.

Find the number such that 5 times the number = 10. Method let x be the number, so that 5x=10. Then divide this equation by 5, so x=2 is the solution. Answer: the number =2.

Solve: Find the number such that a) 3 times the number = 15, b) Twice the number = 280 c) 6 times the number =42, d) 12 times the number = 30: Answer 12x = 30, so dividing by 6, 2x = 5,

x =5/2=2.5, the number is 2.5

Solve: a) 10 x the number = 55, b) 8 x the number = 44

Solve: a) 9 x the number – 4 = 50; 9x - 4 = 50 add 4

9x-4+4 = 50+4

9x = 54; divide by 9

x = 6. The number is 6.   Proof= 9x6-4= 50 so x=6 is correct

Solve: 8 x the number – 6 = 50

10 x the number + 4 = 144

Nonfiction

SIXTEEN
AQUARIUMS

Aquariums are glass containers framed with metal sidings. Aquariums are used for fish and small crustaceans to live n. Aquarium containers come in different sizes. Some aquariums are glass bowls.

Chinese restaurants usually have large aquariums to display small, tropical fish as well as goldfish and carps. Pebbles and coral rocks generally are placed at the bottom of aquariums. Sea plants and kelp are put into aquariums. Fish can hide inside coral and rock enclosures if they don't want to be seen readily.

There is one of the largest aquariums in Monterey, California in Cannery Row near the Monterey Harbor. Sharks and a variety of ocean fish and shell life live in this enormous aquarium. Many tourists and other visitors come to Monterey to this famous aquarium.

In Spain, along the harbor is another very large aquarium where a wide variety of sea life is kept. Sea turtles are healed of diseases at this new aquarium. Their shells are cleansed of barnacles and parasites which cause diseases in sea turtles. Sharks and whales live in this enormous aquarium.

Chinese people usually have aquariums in Chinese restaurants. They believe fish bring them good luck in their restaurants.

Aquariums may be in doctor's waiting rooms and even in some business establishments.

Pet shops may sell aquarium equipment. Fish food can be purchased at pet shops. Fish may be purchased at pet shops. A variety of tropical fish add to the beauty of an aquarium. Sea plants can be obtained at certain pet shops.

You can purchase aquariums at pet shops and create your own aquarium. You can purchase all the supplies usually at a pet shop for your aquarium. You should clean the water out regularly in your aquarium. The water temperature should be kept at the temperature fish can accept and be comfortable in. The proper temperature is important so fish will live longer and remain healthy.

Aquariums are popular around the world. Many people enjoy looking at fish moving around in aquariums.

Nonfiction

SEVENTEEN
OCEAN CURRENTS

Ocean currents are created by gravitational pull and wind. Ocean currents are necessary so ocean water can continue to move in the ocean. Moving water is healthier and fresher.

Stagnant, ocean water is not clean. Pollution has accumulated in the ocean. Two-thirds of the Earth is covered with ocean water. Ocean currents roll to many shores around the world. These ocean currents affect landscapes. Beaches have been formed because ocean water causes soil to turn into bleached out sand.

Ocean currents move at different speeds because of the movement of the Earth. The Earth is round and is moving around on its axis every 24 hours. This constant movement affects the way the ocean moves. Ocean currents are much more powerful during ocean storms. Waves rise up very swiftly causing strong ocean currents. Boats and ships at sea must be careful especially during storms at sea. Boats can capsize and ships have sunk because of violent storms at sea.

Ocean currents are necessary so ocean water can continue to move and to generate life. Sea life such as fish, sea plants and coral life depend on moving water generated by ocean currents.

The ocean moves back and forth and has ebb tides. We depend on the ocean for food and moisture. Clouds are created from the evaporation of ocean water. Ocean currents eventually evaporate causing clouds to develop. Clouds eventually cause rain to fall back down to the Earth so plants and animals will have water. Ocean currents are valuable when they move back and forth in balance to help nature on Earth.

Tsunamis are tidal waves caused by earthquakes and severe wind currents. When ocean currents are severely out of balance they can be harmful. Red kelp is accumulating in the oceans. Ocean currents move the red kelp around. Red kelp pollutes the ocean. When ocean currents cause red kelp to float around in the ocean the red kelp keeps moving in large groups. Red kelp can not be eaten because it can be harmful.

As long as ocean currents exist the currents will affect life in the ocean and on land especially near seashores. We need to take care of the oceans and land on earth to promote balance, equilibrium and harmony.

The most important ocean currents affecting global climate changes are the El Nino and La Nina currents. An El Nino current can result in a great amount of winter rainfall on the West Coast of North America and some other zones and cause droughts in other zones. A La Nina ocean current can cause droughts on the Northern Hemisphere western states and nations.

During most years the ocean currents off of most of South America is a cold flow from Antarctica that causes dry weather along that coastline and many droughts in the western part of the Northern Hemisphere. This condition is the La Nina current. The prevailing trade winds blow warm equatorial and subtropical ocean waters away from North, Central and South America. Colder ocean currents create arid landscape along much of the Western United States and northwestern Mexico, while warm ocean currents result in dense, green vegetation along the East Coasts at the same latitudes.

Many floods, long rainstorms and tropical storms appear along the west coasts of North and South America when the prevailing winds reverse directions during El Nino. Instead of trade winds moving air and water toward the west, the winds usually blow toward the American continents during La Nina. This prevailing wind direction blows warm, tropical ocean water from equatorial regions toward South and Central America to create wet autumns and winters. More hurricanes often result. Ocean temperatures can be ten or more degrees above normal along many coasts. Peru's usual, dry, desert, coastal climate becomes warm, wet, humid and tropical. Extreme prevailing weather changes occur in much of the world during La Nina.

Air and water temperatures, humidity and dryness as well as wet and arid climates are not caused by the distance from the equator. Warm or cool ocean currents cause these differences in climate and scenery. The warm Gulf Stream from an equatorial zone causes the warm, tropical, humid and rainy climate of Florida and the Bahamas. However, the same distance from the equator on the West Coast is considered arid, usually dry, and cooler from the cold ocean current from the north. The subtropical East Coast is entirely dense, green natural vegetation. The same distance from the equator on the West Coast is mostly deserts and barren landscapes because of the cool ocean current. Warm ocean currents bring wet summers and monsoon rain patterns. Cool ocean currents bring dry summers.

Fiction

EIGHTEEN
THE PEARL NECKLACE

Miriam Brown loved jewelry. She collected earrings, necklaces, bracelets, rings and broaches. She liked to go to different jewelry stores and department stores to look for new jewelry. Miriam even went to goodwill stores and thrift shops to select and buy jewelry. She wore necklaces, bracelets, earrings and rings frequently whenever she went out to activities and events.

One day Miriam went to a jewelry shop across town. She browsed around in this shop for awhile. She looked into glass cases. She spotted a beautiful pearl necklace. This necklace cost $2,500. Miriam usually spent small amounts of money for jewelry. She asked the proprietor if she could try on this precious necklace.

The proprietor took the pearl necklace out of the glass case for Miriam to try on. The proprietor placed the pearl necklace around Miriam's neck. She closed the fastener on the necklace. Miriam looked in a larger counter mirror at this lovely, pearl necklace. It looked magnificent around her neck.

Miriam thought about the fastener on the necklace. Miriam looked in a larger counter mirror at this lovely, pearl necklace. It looked magnificent around her neck.

Miriam thought about the price of this pearl necklace. She couldn't afford to pay $2,500 for this necklace. The proprietor told her that this necklace could be paid for in monthly installments.

Each monthly installment payment was $100. In two years the necklace would be paid for. Miriam thought about this payment plan. She wanted a real pearl necklace.

Finally, after thinking it over, Miriam decided to make monthly payments for two years. The pearl necklace would be kept in a storage place at the jewelry store until the last payment was made. Miriam left the store. She would mail each payment to the jewelry store.

Each month Miriam wrote a check for $100. She knew she would have to wait two years before she would be able to wear the pearl necklace. After making one year's payments Miriam was becoming quite restless about wearing the pearl necklace. She found out that the pearls were gathered from oysters near Japan in the ocean. However, Miriam really was tired of waiting to wear the pearl necklace.

Miriam happened to come into a jewelry store that displayed pearl necklaces which looked good. The pearls looked real. Miriam found out the pearls were not real. These imitation pearl necklaces only cost $35. Miriam realized that she had already spent $1,200. She didn't want to spend anymore money for the real pearl necklace. She decided to stop making anymore payments.

Miriam tried on several imitation pearl necklaces. She thought these pearl necklaces were very attractive. She decided to buy a $35 imitation pearl necklace. She wore her new, imitation, pearl necklace before she walked out of the jewelry store.

Miriam went back to the jewelry store where she was making monthly payments. She told the proprietor she wanted her $1,200 back which she had paid during the year. The proprietor called the owner of the jewelry store to ask what to do about Miriam's request.

The owner of the jewelry store told the employee to tell Miriam that she had signed a payment to make all the monthly payments. The owner told the store employee to tell Miriam that she could not have the $1,200 back.

Miriam became angry because she thought it wasn't fair that she couldn't receive her $1,200 back. After all, she didn't have the real pearl necklace. She felt she should have her money back. The proprietor told her that she couldn't return the $1,200.

Miriam felt that she had wasted $1,200 unnecessarily. She felt frustrated and cheated. She wanted to take her case to a local court. However, she had signed a paper that would weaken her case.

Several weeks later Miriam went to the local courthouse. She brought her written report into the courtroom. There were approximately 30 other people in the courtroom. Miriam waited patiently to state her case to a courtroom judge.

Judge Johnson called Miriam Brown to come up to state her case. Miriam brought her written case to the stand. The judge asked Miriam to state her case. Miriam stood there and stated, "I went to the Addison Jewelry store in town a year ago. I purchased a pearl necklace for $2,500. I was told I could pay $100 a month until the $2,500 was paid. I didn't see anything in writing that stated I couldn't get my payments back if I changed my mind about purchasing the pearl necklace. I asked to be refunded the $1,200 which I paid during the year."

Judge Johnson asked, "Did the jewelry proprietor tell you verbally that you could not receive the $1,200 back?" Miriam was facing the judge. She said, "The proprietor didn't make it clear that I couldn't be refunded the $1,200. I have never been able to wear the pearl necklace. My hard earned money has been wasted. I no longer want the pearl necklace. I want my $1,200 back!"

Judge Johnson knew Miriam was upset and felt it was unfair for her to pay $1,200 and still not be able to wear this necklace. Judge Johnson studied her written report and he thought about what she stated to him. He then made a decision. He stated, "It is my understanding that you signed an agreement which you did not understand. You didn't read the fine print about not being able to receive your monthly payments back if you changed your mind. The proprietor didn't clarify verbally what was expected from what you have told me. I have decided that you should be refunded $600.

Miriam realized the judge was giving her fifty percent of her money back. This was better than losing all of the money. Miriam had to accept Judge Johnson's decision. The Addison Jewelry Store was required to refund Miriam $600. She had to accept that she had lost $600. She learned a lesson that she would read the fine print on written agreements in the future. She decided never to invest a lot of money in jewelry. She accepted imitation jewelry because it was not expensive.

NINETEEN
IMAGINE IF---

Imagine if you were very wealthy. What would you do with millions of dollars to spend? How would you invest your money? Many individuals who acquire wealth spend money for expensive homes, expensive cars and boats and expensive clothes.

Wealthy people can afford to eat out at very expensive restaurants and resorts. They are able to travel readily around the world. Wealthy people are able to travel in private planes and helicopters. They usually can take the time to travel in first class style because they can afford to spend a lot of money for different accommodations and travel arrangements.

Wealthy people generally have the freedom to invest their money into different projects, programs and financial investments. Imagine if you had millions of dollars to spend any way you wanted to.

Wealthy individuals can afford to help many impoverished people who need food, clothes and shelter. They are able to provide apartment complexes for poor people who need comfortable places to live.

Wealthy people are able to contribute money for educational enrichment programs, facilities and special equipment. Needy children are able to receive a better education. If more wealthy people donated money to help children in the lower, economic group they could receive an education. Our children on Earth can improve if our young people are well educated to help improve life on Earth. A good education can make a difference in the world. Living conditions can be improved on our planet if we are well educated to learn how to improve our way of life.

Wealthy people can contribute to the arts. They can afford to buy expensive artwork such as rare paintings, sculptures and tapestries. Wealthy individuals can afford to donate money to the theaters in big cities and to universities and colleges. Large donations help to keep stage play theaters open. Wealthy people are able to support theaters by donating a lot of money for costumes, stage props and sets and for directors' stage play instructions. Many theaters are supported by wealthy donors.

Imagine if you never had to worry about money. Imagine if you could do just about anything you wanted to do because you had a lot of money. You would feel free to spend money for many reasons. You could have several vacation homes. You would be able to go on vacations when you want to have a change from the regular, daily routine.

Life can be a lot easier when the stress of making enough money at a 40 hour a week job is eliminated. When all bills are paid for you feel better because you don't have to worry about paying them. Having a lot of accumulated money in savings is useful to have to take care of your needs and desires. You can imagine what you want to do and do it.

TWENTY
ORGANS OF THE HUMAN BODY

We have vital organs in our body. Essential organs are the heart, brain, lungs, stomach, veins, arteries, intestines, esophagus, bowels, kidney's, liver, bladder and private parts. We must have these organs in order to stay alive.

Other organs in the body are the appendix, spleen, urethra, tonsils, muscles beneath the skin, and regular tissue in the body. Every organ has specific functions to help maintain the human body. Each organ has an important purpose for existing in the human body.

The brain is the most important organ in the human body. The brain is a large muscle-like organ which stores the memory, messages for all the nerves and cells in the human body. Thoughts are stored in the brain. The heart is very vital. It is a muscle which pumps the blood into arteries and veins in the human body. Without the heart to pump blood, a person would not be able to live in a human body.

The brain is the most important organ in the human body. The brain is a large muscle-like organ which stores the memory, messages for all the nerves and cells in the human body. Thoughts are stored in the brain. The heart is very vital. It is a muscle which pumps the blood into arteries and veins in the human body. Without the heart to pump blood, a person would not be able to live in a human body.

Lungs are necessary so oxygen can be sent into all the cells of the body. The lungs receive oxygen and the oxygen is released into the blood stream and into the cells of the body. The stomach dissolves food particles. Food is churned around in the stomach. Energy and substance from digested food go into the bloodstream to bring nourishment to the cells of the body.

Food, which is no longer used, goes into the intestines. Waste matter goes into the rectum to harden. This hardened, wasted matter becomes stools which pass out of the body as solid matter. Urine is liquid which is no longer needed. Urine passes out of the bladder through the urethra duct of the body. Everyone is required to eliminate unnecessary waste matter out of the body regularly.

The arteries carry fresh blood into the cells. Old blood is carried away through the veins to be cleansed by the heart. Blood is necessary to carry oxygen, food and energy into the body.

The liver is a vital organ. It maintains the life force in the body. Without the liver the body would not survive. The kidneys clean out the impurities in the urine. The kidneys help to purify the bloodstream. The kidneys are necessary to help a person function properly. The bladder stores the urine. The urine is released from the bladder and goes into the urethra and out of the body. Without a bladder there would be no place to store the urine.

The appendix stores impurities and toxins. The appendix flushes the impurities and toxins out of the blood stream. The spleen also stores impurities. Body tissues and muscles are necessary in the body to hold the body together.

All body organs help work in harmony and function to serve the body. Each organ must function properly so human beings can be healthy. Each organ carries out its purpose. People who maintain healthy organs usually live longer lives.

Fiction

TWENTY-ONE
TAKING ACTION

People take action in order to resolve problems and issues. It is important to act wisely and quickly about serious concerns. A person may take action on against people who abuse animals. They may take action against people who invade their privacy. People take action against people who treat other people abusively. Taking action means doing something about injustices, wrongdoings and problems.

Roxanne Dixon was facing a problem. She had lost her job as a receptionist for a large, business firm. Roxanne was only 33 years old. She could only receive unemployment benefits for six months. She went looking for a new job. It was difficult to find another position as a receptionist.

Roxanne felt she had been fired from the receptionist job unfairly. Someone had gossiped about her and lied about here causing Roxanne to lose her job. Roxanne decided to take action against the individuals who gossiped about her. She filed a written complaint in the personnel department at the business firm where she had been employed.

Roxanne stated the false accusations against her in writing. She explained why the accusations were false. Someone had accused Roxanne of being constantly late to work. Roxanne stated that she was on time to work regularly. Someone else said that Roxanne was unpleasant to clients and customers who came to the business firm for appointments. Roxanne presented at least 10 witnesses who stated she was pleasant and professional as a receptionist. Roxanne submitted her complaint and report hoping to be reinstated to her position as a receptionist at the same business firm.

Roxanne was given an appointment to come to the director of employment at the business firm to voice her complaint openly to the employment director. The director of employment at the business firm called Roxanne in for a meeting. She voiced her complaints and evidence regarding her case. The director listened closely to her case about how unfair it was that she was fired from her receptionist position at this business firm. He asked her several questions about why certain people had gossiped maliciously about her. Roxanne stated that these individuals were jealous of her and they were her enemies. They gossiped to cause her trouble.

The director thought about what Roxanne stated in her complaint. She had pleaded also to get her job back as a receptionist at the business firm. The director said he would contact Roxanne soon to let her know what his decision was.

Roxanne thanked the director for listening to her case. She left the director's office and went back to her apartment. Roxanne waited several days before she received a call from the employment director. He asked Roxanne to come back to his office. Roxanne was anxious to hear what his decision was. She got into her car and drove to the business firm. She walked into the business firm and went directly to the personnel office.

The employment director greeted Roxanne when she came to his office. Roxanne sat down across from the director's desk. Mr. Costa, the director, looked at Roxanne warmly. He said, "I have thought over what you stated and voiced in your complaint. I investigated what happened to cause you to be dismissed from your position as a receptionist for this business firm. I found out that individuals who gossiped about you were trying to get you fired deliberately. One individual admitted that she wanted your position as the receptionist. The other person who gossiped also wanted her friend to become the receptionist. I told them that gossiping about you falsely was uncalled for. I told these individuals that they had broken our business policies by gossiping falsely about you. They are no longer working at our business firm because of their unjust actions. I have decided to reinstate you to your position as a receptionist at our business firm.

Roxanne was relieved to hear the director's decision to reinstate her as a receptionist again for this firm. Roxanne was glad that she had taken action by complaining to the director about what had happened to her about her job.

Roxanne thanked the director for reinstating her to her receptionist position again. She had taken action to fight against her enemies. She had won her case. Roxanne went back to work the next day. She continued to work as a receptionist at this business firm for many years.

Fiction

TWENTY-TWO
BEING ADMIRED AND APPRECIATED

P eople like to be admired and appreciated for their accomplishments. Talented individuals are usually admired and appreciated. They become well known for their talents and abilities.

Kit Harrison was admired and appreciated as a comedian and singer. He was tall, dark haired and handsome. He had crystal blue eyes. Kit had a magnetic personality. He was well liked by many people and fans. He dressed in exotic clothing and had interesting hairdos. Kit was very popular as a comedian and singer. Many people continued to admire and appreciate Kit Harrison. Millions of people attended stage presentations where Kit Harrison was performing.

Millie Swanson was a popular actress. She had become a super star over a period of years. She dressed in stylish clothes and had attractive hairdos. She selected beautiful shoes to match her clothes. Millie played major roles in different movies. Many people came to theaters to see the films she was in. Millie Swanson was admired and appreciated by many people and fans.

Larson Smith was a landscaper. He landscaped many gardens in his regional area. Larson was an excellent landscaper. Many people in his regional area called him to come to landscape their gardens. They admired and appreciated the way he contoured and redesigned their gardens. Larson continued to landscape many gardens. He was kept busy with his work because many people requested his services.

Being admired and appreciated is a wonderful experience. We feel better about ourselves and others when we are admired and appreciated.

Nonfiction

TWENTY-THREE
GODLY DEEDS

When a person aspires to serve humanity this is a Godly deed. Each kind and thoughtful action makes a difference. Every thought, word and deed, which is of benefit to oneself and others, is God working in the world.

Humanitarians do godly deeds. A humanitarian reaches out to help others by donating time, energy and even money to serve humanity. Albert Schweitzer went to Africa as a doctor to look after hundreds of Africans. He vaccinated many Africans so they would not get malaria and other diseases. Albert Schweitzer was a Christian. He spread Christianity in Africa where he lived for over twenty years. He played classical and religious music on the organ as well.

Mother Teresa served humanity. She reached out to sick and homeless people in the streets of Madras, India. She gave many impoverished and sick people the will to live and to have faith in God and Jesus Christ. She set an example as a soul who served God by praying for lost souls. She gave hope where there was despair. She inspired others to have faith in God when they lacked faith and belief in God's divine source.

Florence Nightengale served many soldiers during wartime. She established sanitary methods for wounded soldiers. Florence Nightengale established the first hospital so that many sick people would have a place to go to receive proper, medical care. She was kind and helpful to wounded soldiers. Florencee Nightengale had faith in God and she performed Godly deeds.

Each soul who performs Godly deeds can make a difference in the world.

Fiction

TWENTY-FOUR
PERSONAL FEELINGS

Suzanne Hendricks was having a rough time in her personal life. She had met a handsome man who appeared to be about her age. Suzanne was 27 years old. She was attracted to him for different reasons. However, Jeff Adams was engaged to someone else. He was planning to get married soon to a woman he had known for seven years.

Suzanne Hendricks found out that Jeff Adams was engaged. She was very disappointed that Jeff was seriously involved with someone else. Suzanne was in love with Jeff. She wanted him to notice her. It wasn't too late. He wasn't married yet to the gal he was engaged to.

Suzanne decided to pursue Jeff in hopes that he would become interested in her. She went to cafes and restaurants where Jeff usually went to eat meals and to have coffee. Suzanne walked into the Blue Danube Restaurant. She sat down at a booth and she ordered some coffee. She hoped Jeff would show up. Suzanne waited for at least an hour. She read a book while she waited.

Jeff finally showed up at the Blue Danube Restaurant. Fortunately, he was by himself. He saw Suzanne sitting by herself at a booth. Jeff knew Suzanne because he had met her at a party approximately six months ago. He walked over to her and greeted her. He said, "Hi". Suzanne looked at Jeff warmly. She replied, "Hello. How are you?"

Suzanne replied, "I am fine. Would you like to sit here at my table?" Jeff responded, "Sure."

Jeff sat down at Suzanne's table across from her. He noticed her book. So, he asked, "What are you reading?" Suzanne smiled and answered, "I am reading "The King and I." Jeff responded, "I saw the musical version of   The King and I with Debra Kerr and Yul Brenner several years ago." Suzanne said, "I saw the musical when it first came out. The book version is more detailed about Siam and the life of the King of Siam. It is an interesting book."

Suzanne's eyes twinkled with light as she spoke to Jeff. She was glad he was sitting with her and talking to her. She was glad he came to this restaurant by himself. Suzanne decided to communicate about her interests and hobbies. She wanted Jeff to know her better. She hoped he would start showing an interest in her.

Jeff listened attentively to Suzanne while she told him she played tennis, went swimming and hiking. Suzanne said she liked to read and go to discussion groups. Jeff began to show a real interest in Suzanne. He didn't know she was interested in him romantically. Jeff decided to talk about his interests and hobbies.

Jeff mentioned that he liked to go boating, hunting and fishing. He said he didn't read much. He liked to watch television. Jeff liked to eat out and go dancing. Suzanne said she liked to go dancing and to eat out. She continued to look at Jeff warmly with light in her eyes. Jeff realized that Suzanne was interested in him by the way she looked at him. He had ordered a cup of coffee. He finished sipping his coffee.

Jeff stood up and said, "Take care. I have to go meet my fiancée. She is waiting for me." Suzanne tried not to look disappointed because Jeff was leaving especially to go see his fiancée. Suzanne said, "Nice seeing you." Jeff smiled. Then he said, "Well, good bye." He left the restaurant.

Suzanne sat there in the Blue Danube Restaurant feeling despondant. She realized that she had little chance to become romantically involved with Jeff. He would be married in a few weeks. Suzanne took her book and left the restaurant after she paid for her coffee. She walked down the street to the nearby beach.

As Suzanne walked on the beach she felt the warm sand on her feet. The wet sand was smooth as she walked into the ocean. Waves splashed to the shore over her bare feet. She thought about Jeff.

Several weeks later Suzanne was shopping in a dress shop for a new dress and coat. While she was there looking at clothes she saw someone who knew Jeff and his fiancée, Carol. Her name was Silvia. Silvia walked over to Suzanne and said, "Hi Suzanne. Have you found anything to buy yet?" Suzanne replied. "Not yet." Suzanne kept looking in the dress racks for dresses to try on.

Silvia looked at Suzanne sadly and said, "Did you hear about Carol?" Suzanne looked at Silvia with a curious expression and replied, "No. What happened?" Silvia said, "Carol was in a serious car accident. She is in the Emergency Ward at the hospital. She is not expected to live." Suzanne looked shocked. She said, "I hadn't heard about Carol's accident. I'm sorry she was badly injured."

Silvia responded. "Carol's neck was broken. She also has a serious concussion. She is in a coma." Suzanne asked, "Has Jeff been told about Carol's car accident?" Silvia replied, "Jeff knows about her car accident. He probably is at the hospital right now to be by her side. I don't know if other visitors are allowed to go see her." Suzanne replied, "Probably not if Carol is in the Emergency Ward." Silvia said, "I hope she doesn't die. I have to go now. Bye." Silvia walked away and left the store.

Suzanne thought about Carol. She wondered how critical Carol's accident was. She continued to look for an attractive dress and matching coat. She found a beautiful, turquoise dress with gold trim. She also located a matching, gold coat. Suzanne took these items to the dressing room and tried them on. The dress and coat looked very attractive on Suzanne. She decided to purchase them.

When Suzanne left the dress shop with her packaged clothes she decided to drive over to the hospital to check about Carol's condition. Once she walked into the Emergency Ward area she asked a nurse about Carol. The nurse said Carol had died several hours ago. Suzanne knew Jeff must have found out already that his fiancée had died. Suzanne looked around the Emergency Ward for Jeff. He wasn't there.

So, Suzanne left the hospital and went home. She decided to call Jeff. She dialed his phone number. Jeff answered his phone. Suzanne said, "Hello Jeff. This is Suzanne." Jeff replied, "Hello." Suzanne continued, "I'm sorry to hear about Carol. What an unexpected turn of events." Jeff sounded despondent. He said, "Carol is gone. I didn't expect this to happen. I feel so bad about what happened to her."

Suzanne took the opportunity to console Jeff. She said, "If I can help in any way please let me be here for you especially now." Jeff replied, "I need to be alone for now." Suzanne responded. "I understand." Jeff answered. "Thanks for calling." Suzanne said, "Let me know if you need a companion. I'm available. Bye." Suzanne hung up.

Several months went by. Jeff didn't call Suzanne. She thought he was in mourning so she didn't call him again. One day Suzanne was walking on the beach alone. As she walked farther down the beach she saw Jeff in the distance. She kept walking towards him. Finally she was close to Jeff.

Suzanne greeted Jeff warmly on the beach. She said, "Hello Jeff. How are you?" Jeff looked at Suzanne with half of a smile. He replied, "O.K. I guess." Suzanne didn't want to remind Jeff about Carol's death. Instead, she spoke cheerfully. She said, "It's a beautiful day! The sun is about to set. The colors are beautiful near the horizon." Jeff responded, "It is beautiful. Do you walk on the beach often?" Suzanne answered, "I usually walk on the beach several times a week. How about you?" Jeff replied, "I walk on the beach usually once a week." Suzanne responded, "Good. I'm glad you enjoy walking on the beach. I am ready to leave. I have had my walk. Would you like to join me for a cup of coffee at the Beach Café?"

Jeff replied, "A cup of coffee sounds good. I will join you." So, Suzanne and Jeff walked together to the Beach Café. They entered this café and sat at a window which was near the harbor. They could see a view of the bay. They ordered cappacino with cream on the top of the cappacino to add to this drink. As they sipped their cappacino they continued to become more acquainted. Jeff revealed how he felt about his life. He spoke about his childhood and his parents, brothers and sisters. She found out that Jeff was the younger child in his family. His parents had traveled around the world. He had two older sisters and another older brother.

Suzanne listened carefully to Jeff talk about his past. She found out that he had traveled around the world with his parents and siblings. Jeff knew a lot about different places. He was interesting to listen to because of his adventures and descriptions about scenic places. Suzanne felt even more in love with Jeff as she listened to him describe his traveling experiences. He had lived an interesting life.

Jeff mentioned that he was very much in love with Carol. He was having difficulty in adjusting to her untimely death. Suzanne understood how Jeff felt. She felt sad because she knew he was still mourning Carol's death. She wanted to tell him how much she loved him. However, this wasn't the appropriate time to tell him how she felt about him. She decided to remain silent about her personal feelings for him. She hoped someday that Jeff would be ready for another romantic relationship. She decided to wait for the right time to have a romantic relationship with him.

Nonfiction

TWENTY-FIVE
BIG CITIES

Big cities are usually noisy, busy places where there are many people, buildings and residential zones. There are people walking in the streets, driving by in cars, trucks and riding public buses. Many public buildings, apartments and homes are built very close together. There are usually many cultural things to do in big cities such as going to museums, art galleries, department stores, shops, restaurants, public libraries and public malls and parks.

Big cities provide many activities and events. There are theaters and amusement centers. Some big cities are near the ocean. There are long beaches stretching along the coastlines. Tall buildings stand out in the harbor. Skyscrapers are seen in many big cities. Many people live very close together. Yet, they are strangers.

Large bridges usually connect a transportation system between one city and another city. Port cities have large harbors where large ships and boats are anchored. Imports and exports are brought on large vessels to trade and exchange goods and supplies. Port cities are needed so people can travel readily by sea in passenger ships and boats. There usually are many restaurants and shops near harbors to provide food, trading, shopping and entertainment.

There are big cities all around the world. Some big cities are New York City in New York, San Francisco and Los Angeles in California, Chicago in Illinois, Phoenix in Arizona, London in England, Dublin in Ireland, Rome in Italy, Naples in Italy, Paris in France, Barcelona in Spain, Madrid in Spain, Mexico City in Mexico, Brasilia in Brazil and more. These big cities offer cultural and historical stimulation. Many people travel to these big cities for a vacation because they offer a wide variety of things to do.

Fiction

TWENTY-SIX
DESERT EXPERIENCES

Deserts are hot, dry and arid places with mainly rolling sand and some desert plants such as cactus and desert brush and sage brushes, etc. The temperature rises from 100 to 130 degrees. It gets very hot during the day and quite cold at night when the sun is no longer shining in the fall and winter sky. In the summer it sometimes is over 90 degrees all night in some deserts. There are desert snakes, scorpions, lizards, toads and desert insects.

Shelley and Stuart Rogers decided to travel in the desert. They packed their camping equipment in their car. The next morning they began their trip from Escondido to the Mojave Desert in California. They traveled for hundreds of miles inland until they came to the desert. It was very hot in the Mojave Desert.

Stuart and Shelley stopped in the desert near a big yucca tree. They stepped out of their car and stood in the shade of this desert tree. Yucca blossoms were growing on the yucca trees because it was Spring time. The air was dry but smelled fresh. There was no pollution lingering in the desert air. Stuart and Shelley decided to unpack their car. They set up a tent and placed their bed rolls and camping equipment in the tent.

The Rogers went for a walk in the Mojave Desert. Some sagebrush was tumbling across the sandy terrain. Desert toads and lizards were crawling through desert brush and small, desert plants. Stuart and Shelley noticed several gray snakes with speckled designs meandering on the desert ground. They stopped to watch them moving in and out of the brush and saw them crawl under some rocks into the shady area.

Stuart and Shelly kept walking across the desert in the heat. They were wearing straw hats and they wore causal, cotton clothes and tennis shoes to be more comfortable. They observed desert insects crawling in the sand and on desert plants. There were desert ants, centipedes, sow bugs and scorpions. Shelley observed several centipedes mingling in the hot sand. They left imprints as they moved around. Scorpions appeared harmless. However, Shelley and Stuart knew scorpions could suddenly sting sharply to poison their victims.

Shelley and Stuart continued to walk through the desert. Suddenly, a desert rodent appeared in the distance. It sniffed some desert plants. It was looking for food. It chased a snake which quickly crawled under some rocks. The rodent was unable to catch the snake once it hid under some rocks. The rodent noticed Shelley and Stuart walking in the desert. It darted away quickly.

Stuart and Shelley were hot from the piercing sun. They kept walking. The time went by and the sun began to move across the sky. It began to get dark. Stuart and Shelley decided to turn around and head back to their tent. However, they turned in the wrong direction as they walked along. They stopped and rested under a yucca tree. It got darker. They decided to continue to walk. They weren't able to find their tent.

The Rogers became worried because they realized they were lost. They were tired, thirsty and hungry. They were away from the direction of the sun and kept looking for their tent and car. Finally, Stuart spotted their car and tent in the distance. Stuart and Shelley walked towards their car. It took another thirty minutes to reach it. They decided to go into their tent to rest and drink some water.

While the Rogers were in their tent the sun went down. It became very dark outside. Shelley turned on a flashlight in order to see. Stuart and Shelley ate some packed sandwiches and drank more water. They ate oranges for dessert, It was time to go to bed for the night. Before Stuart and Shelley went to sleep they decided to go outside their tent to watch the twinkling stars come out. They saw the North Star, the big Dipper, the Little Dipper and the Pleiades. The Moon appeared and it looked very bright as it moved across the sky.

Then Shelley and Stuart went back into their tent to bed down for the night. During the night they heard coyotes howling. Shelley worried that coyotes might come over to their tent. She was unable to sleep. She was sunburned from the hot, burning sunlight during the day time. She felt uncomfortable. She thought about the experiences she had during her walk in the desert during the day. She recalled the rodents, snakes, toads, lizards and insects along her hike with Stuart.

Early the next morning Shelley got up as the sunrise appeared near the horizon. Stuart woke up beside Shelley. The temperature was around 72 degrees in the early morning at 6:30 A.M. Shelley and Stuart were already dressed in their casual clothes which they wore all night in case of an emergency. Shelley prepared fruit and buttered bread for breakfast. She poured some orange juice into two glasses. Stuart and Shelley ate their breakfast.

Shelley rolled up the bedrolls. Stuart helped her take down the tent. They packed their car. It was time to go. Stuart drove their car across the Mojave Desert towards their home in Palm Springs, California. While they were traveling back across the desert they suddenly encountered thousands of flying locusts which were grasshoppers, coming towards them. The locusts swarmed around their moving car. The locusts were eating all the vegetation as they moved in their direction.

The swarming locusts were so thick that they caused Stuart to stop his car. Locusts covered the windshield of the Rogers' car. Stuart could not see out the windshield. Stuart and Shelley closed all the windows in their car to keep the locusts out. They waited for them to move on so they could continue their journey back to Escondido. The locusts finally moved on to eat more vegetation in the desert. It was very hot in the car with the windows up.

Once the locusts were gone Stuart stepped out of the car and cleaned the windshield off. He got back in the car and continued driving. He came to a public restroom at a rest stop. Both Stuart and Shelley needed to go to the restroom to use the toilets. Then they walked into the public restrooms. Hundreds of locusts were everywhere. Dead locusts were in the toilets.

Stuart and Shelley were unable to use the toilets. They finally went outside and eliminated there despite the fact that someone might see them. Fortunately, no one else was around. Then they got back into their car and traveled out of the desert.

The Rogers were relieved to leave the Mojave Desert. They journeyed back to Escondido, California. When they returned home, Stuart and Shelley were able to relax and enjoy the many modern conveniences in their home.

Nonfiction

TWENTY-SEVEN
THE MISSING LINK

In life there are missing links. Many mysteries occur and many unexplainable experiences happen. Peopled wonder why they are experiencing unusual accounts which cause suffering and unhappiness. Many bizarre occurrences may take place for unforeseen reasons.

Karen Carpenter, a well known American country and ballad music singer and movie star, became famous. Yet, she was so concerned about her appearance she stopped eating enough food to stay alive. She eventually died from starvation. Why did she allow her body to be depleted of necessary nutrients? Karen Carpenter worried that she would not remain a popular singer in the top ten if she gained weight and didn't look extremely slender. The missing link was in Karen's mind. She was very critical about becoming plump. She became unhealthy because of her desire to look slender. Unfortunately, Karen died because of this false belief in being extremely slender.

Elvis Presley, the King of Rock Music, was very popular as a singer and movie star. He was a sex symbol during his career as a singer and movie star. Yet, Elvis Presley died from an overdose of drugs. He had bodyguards to protect him because he thought he was being "stalked" by certain stalkers. He had a security system installed around his southern mansion estate. Elvis Presley was concerned about his safety. Some investigators think he was working secretly for the FBI.

Elvis Presley may have been able to live much longer if he hadn't been addicted to harmful drugs. He could have felt safer if certain stalkers were not causing him danger. Without the missing link caused by drugs and stalkers, Elvis Presley may have been able to relax and to live a normal life. He deserved his privacy and safety.

John Lennon, who was one of the famous Beatles during the 1960s, led an active, sexual life. He met many women who tried to pursue him. His first wife left him after 6 years of marriage. He had different women affecting his personal life. He eventually married a Japanese woman named Yoko Ono. He began to take harmful drugs. He was hated by certain people. Eventually, John Lennon was shot by a stalker. His life ended tragically. The missing link is why stalkers hunted for him and killed him especially when he had many fans who enjoyed him as a well known singer.

Marilyn Monroe was a very popular movie star in the 1950s and early 1960s. She was a sex symbol around the world. She was married several times. Yet, her marriages didn't last. She had several miscarriages. She never gave birth to a baby. Marilyn began to have difficulties in her marriage. Then Marilyn became involved with America's political leaders. Her life was endangered because she knew too much about confidential issues. It is believed today that Marilyn Monroe was murdered at the age of 36. She became involved with people who enjoyed her sexually. Then these politicians wanted her murdered in order to keep her from talking and gossiping about them. She didn't realize how dangerous these politicians were. They didn't want other people and especially their spouses to know they had been sexually involved with Marilyn Monroe. So, her life was ended tragically because of this dangerous, emotional involvement.

Marilyn Monroe was suffering from spirits haunting her. She listened to voices who affected her erratic behavior. She became unhappy. She depended on the telephone to communicate with certain people. She needed counseling and guidance.

James Dean was a well known movie star in the 1950s. He was very popular. Yet he died in a tragic automobile accident. He had some clashes with other movie stars that he worked with. He was in only five films before he was tragically killed in Paso Robles, California as he drove on Highway 66. James Dean had become a super star very quickly. Unfortunately, his life was ended while he was young. He did not foresee this automobile accident. It was a sudden, tragic death.

Little did Franklin D. Roosevelt realize that he would come down with polio. He eventually became paralyzed. He had to depend on a wheelchair to sit in because he had lost the use of his legs. He had gone swimming in an outdoor pond which caused him to contract polio. He suffered from polio for the rest of his life.

Franklin D. Roosevelt tried to conceal his paralysis from the public when he ran for President of the United States of America. He managed to walk up to the podium to present his Inaugural speech when he was elected as President. He was wearing a metal brace on each of his legs so he could walk. He appeared able to walk and stand while he stood before an audience. Roosevelt depended on his wife, Eleanor, and his family to be supportive.

Franklin D, Roosevelt was able to make important political decisions. He established the New Deal, Boy Scouts and resolved many other political issues. He was an American President for 12 years. He was able to make economic changes to help America to succeed in the world. Yet, in his private life Franklin Roosevelt had experienced unhappiness and stress behind closed doors. He had to resolved the missing link because of his polio which handicapped him.

The missing link is learning to overcome every obstacle in order to resolve serous problems, challenges and hardships in life. Dangers can be avoided. Illnesses can be healed when realistic remedies are applied. The missing link is to develop God control and to develop self realization in order to live happier, healthier lives.

Nonfiction

TWENTY-EIGHT
MATHEMATICS IN DAILY LIFE

Mathematics is used in our daily lives. We write checks to pay people for items we purchase. Then we record how much we spent in our bank ledgers. We subtract each check amount for what we spent. It is necessary to know what money is left in the bank once we record in our bank ledgers.

Money deposited in the bank in our checking and savings account is added into our bank accounts. We subtract the money we take out of the bank to spend for necessary items. We should keep accurate records so we don't bounce any checks. Accurate banking, bookkeeping at the banks is very necessary so banks can keep accurate records of customers' money. Computer records are kept at the banks.

Exchanging money at grocery stores, shops, department stores and market places is a form of mathematics. We need to be able to account money by pennies, nickels, dimes, quarters, fifty cents, one dollar bills, five dollars, ten dollars, one hundred dollars, one thousand dollars, ten thousand dollars and one hundred thousands dollars, etc. We learn to count money accurately. Money is exchanged frequently for goods and services such as food, clothing, household items, etc. Money is traded for merchandise. Accurate counting of money is necessary. If money is not counted properly it can be wasted.

MARVELOUS REFLECTIONS

In school we learned to add, subtract, multiply and divide. We add, subtract, multiply and divide so we can use these mathematical skills in our daily lives. The abacus was used to count with in China during ancient times. The abacus is a group of beads on a wire strand. The Chinese people counted by place value on the abacus.

Prices are labeled on canned and paper wrapped foods, fruits and vegetable stands and boxes labeled with prices by the pound. Money is exchanged for fruits and vegetables based on mathematical methods of using money.

Mathematics will continue to be used in our personal lives and businesses. Our mathematical skills are necessary and valuable.

Nonfiction

TWENTY-NINE
PHENOMENAL RESULTS

The Hubble Telescope was invented in the 1990s and it moves in a shuttle around the Earth. The Hubble Telescope was designed to take photographs of distant galaxies and our galaxy as it orbits the Earth.

Astronomers and scientists have been able to study how galaxies are formed. Different galaxies have different shapes and colors. Black holes have been discovered in different galaxies. A protective shield of energy surrounds our solar system. Astronomers have found out how suns are formed and how they eventually die in different galaxies. Dying suns give out a great deal of energy.

The Voyager has traveled to distant planets and photographs and videos have been taken of the surface of Venus, Mars, Jupiter and moons which revolve around Jupiter. Water has been discovered on Jupiter's moon called Europa. The moon Triton has streaky lines.

The Voyager has photographed close-ups of Mars. The land rover machines on Mars have photographed close-ups. Some former, secret military officers and intelligence agents have stated there is biologically different, underground life on Mars. Pyramids, a sphinx, rectangular buildings, walls, huge stone statues and carvings artificially constructed by a destroyed civilization, have been photographed on Mars. Photos of these ruins from NASA files have been leaked out. Some scientists studying Mars believe it once had oceans and an atmosphere similar to Earth. There is massive evidence of ancient seafloors, rivers and lakes that dried up in a cataclysm. Rock samples have been collected that were hurled to Earth by theoretical, meteor impacts on Mars. Some biologists, examining these stones, believe they contain evidence of primitive life forms. Scientists think water and oxygen can be expanded on Mars so plants can grow by 2020 A.D. This may be a possibility in the future. People from Earth may be able to travel to Mars to live there someday. This phenomenal result may provide future generations a place to survive on Mars especially if the Earth becomes too polluted to live on. NASA has proof there is frozen water on Mars.

We need to take care of our planet. By stopping water, air and soil pollution we can preserve the Earth for future generations. We need to protect our environment in order to live here. Phenomenal awareness will help humanity to find ways to save our planet Earth.

Fiction

THIRTY
WE HAVE MANY OPPORTUNITIES

We have many opportunities in life. It is up to each person to pursue new opportunities and goals to fulfill his or her life. Different lifestyles affect our way of thinking and development of attitudes. We can make intelligent choices. Our choices affect what we experience and learn about in our daily lives.

Charmine Gallager wanted to live an adventurous and dynamic life. She had an opportunity to be creative. She enjoyed singing, dancing, painting and photography. She went to college and majored in elementary education with a focus in Child Study and Child Development. Charmine also studied Art. She painted landscapes, ocean scenes and flowers. She learned as much about Art as she could so that she would become a fine artist.

Charmine learned to play the piano from the age of 5 on. She became an accomplished pianist within 7 years. By the age of 12 she played many classical pieces by well known, classical composers. Charmine performed in piano recitals. She performed in school programs and at church. Audiences appreciated the way Charmine performed as a pianist.

Charmine did her best at almost everything she chose to learn to do. She accepted many opportunities. She wanted to learn as much about life as she could day by day, month by month and year by year. Charmine enjoyed learning many things. She was enthusiastic about experiencing new interests and hobbies. She realized that life should be lived to the fullest. She lived a fulfilled and happy life.

We all have opportunities to develop our abilities, talents, interests and hobbies. We can further our education and knowledge about this world and outer space. There are many cultural activities and events to participate in. We should continue to grow and develop our awareness about a wide variety of experiences throughout our lives.

Nonfiction

THIRTY-ONE
SPELLING CORRECTLY

Spelling correctly is important in order to produce professional writing. Learning to spell requires the ability to recognize word parts, syllables, prefixes, suffixes, gerunds, plural words and plural endings.

Any word which is difficult to spell should be looked up in Webster's Dictionary. Begin with the first three letters of the word. Then continue to find the correct word. Check the word carefully to be sure it is the correct word.

When you write a letter, a report, a short story, a novel, a stage play or screenplay, be sure to reread each sentence very carefully. Check every word closely. Correct every misspelled word. Whatever you write should be accurate.

Many words are learned when you write frequently. New words are used and descriptive words may be difficult to spell. Use a Thesaurus to select a variety of descriptive words. Spelling correctly is important so readers can understand what they are reading.

Nonfiction

THIRTY-TWO
THE COUNTRY FAIR

The County Fair is a big event every year. The County Fair moves from county to county. Many exciting activities and entertainment take place at County Fairs.

When the County Fair comes to Paso Robles and Santa Maria, California many people pay to enter the fairgrounds before they are allowed to enter the County Fair.

Once you enter the County Fair there are a variety of exhibits available to look at. Exhibits are displayed by 4-H members, Boy Scouts, Campfire Girls, Girl Scouts, Elks Club, Rodeo Club, Women's Club and artists in the County.

Flower exhibits are arranged in a special room. Many flowers are visible to enjoy. Flower arrangements are presented by flower arrangers. Flowers are carefully placed one by one into a large vase or other container. Each flower is carefully arranged by color and shape with background leaves. Audiences observe how flowers are arranged.

There is an exhibit room for modern conveniences in the home. Demonstrations are presented in cooking and use of kitchen utensils, pots, pans and casserole dishes. Someone may demonstrate how to make peanut butter or salads. Someone may demonstrate how to mop floors with a new and better mop.

Massage equipment may be available. Wrist watches may be displayed. Foot vibrators may be demonstrated. Cosmetic make-up may be demonstrated to show how to use facial make-up. Solar energy may be demonstrated to show how solar energy is produced.

Giant horses and enormous pigs may be seen. People pay extra money to see them. There may be ostrich races or pony races. Singers with guitars may perform. Dancers may perform in groups. They may wear costumes to add color and flair to their performance. A variety of vocal and instrumental performers may perform on stages.

There are booths arranged in a special area in the fairgrounds where fast foods are served. Hot dogs, popcorn, Mexican burritos, hamburgers, French fries, cold sodas, coffee and water are served. Chinese food such as chow mein, chop suey and egg rolls may be served. Fried or baked chicken and even turkey legs may be served. Cotton candy and taffy are served as well.

There is a section for games, a Ferris Wheel and Merry-Go-Round may be available to ride on. Darts may be aimed at targets .Prizes are awarded to winners who win games. Children and adults enjoy games and rides.

Many people come from far away to enjoy County Fairs. People usually stay for many hours to enjoy the County Fair. They look forward to attending the County Fair again next year.

Nonfiction

THIRTY-THREE
FARMERS MARKET

Farmers Market has existed for many years. Farmers Market began in towns and cities. Farmers bring fresh fruits and vegetables to a specific, open place so people can purchase them in an outdoor market. However, nuts and grain are also sold at the Farmers Market.

Many people have an opportunity to select organic, fresh fruits and vegetables farmers have gathered to bring to the open markets. Farmers Market takes place in Arroyo Grande, San Luis Obispo, Paso Robles, Santa Maria, Morro Bay, Los Osos and Cambria in California. Los Angeles and San Francisco have Farmers Markets generally every week.

Farmers Markets began in ancient times. Farmers walked or rode wagons to market places on a daily basis to bring fresh fruits, vegetables, grains and nuts to be sold while they were fresh. There was no refrigeration before the 19th Century. A variety of fruit such as oranges, cantaloupes, apples, pears, watermelons, peaches, plums, pineapples, bananas, grapes and lemons are displayed in the market place. Fresh vegetables are lettuce, cabbages, tomatoes, potatoes, squash, zucchini, carrots, green, red and yellow peppers, onions, celery, radishes, kale, cucumbers, pumpkins, cauliflower, corn, string beans, etc. Beans were in bags and boxes, etc. Beans were in bags and boxes such as pinto beans, lima beans, barley, black-eyed Susans, navy beans and red beans.

A variety of nuts are in sacks and boxes such as peanuts, hazel nuts, cashew nuts, soya nuts, walnuts, pine nuts, almonds and pecans. Wheat flour and rye flour are sold in bags and sacks.

Farmers Market has become a traditional event in Europe, Asia and America. Open market places may continue to exist year by year on a weekly basis, in different towns, villages and cities.

Nonfiction

THIRTY-FOUR
OUR FAVORITE RESTAURANTS

In today's world many restaurants exist. Many people like to eat out. People have the opportunity to select their favorite restaurants.

Some people prefer to go to a restaurant with American food. Some people enjoy going to Chinese restaurants because of the variety of Chinese cuisine. Other people enjoy going to Italian restaurants to eat pizza, spaghetti, pasta and egg plant parmesan.

Other restaurants may be preferred such as Thai restaurants because the food is spicy and different. Korean restaurants appeal to some people. Vegetable and rice dishes are tasty. Japanese food is prepared by frying and dipping vegetables into a special dough to fry the vegetables. The vegetables are quite delicious when they are prepared in fried dough.

You may select a restaurant for a variety of reasons. The food may be spicy. The prices may be reasonable. There may be a variety of food served. There may be many selections on the menu. The restaurant may be decorated in an interesting manner. The servers may be efficient and friendly. These variety of reasons may be why certain restaurants are our favorite places to eat. We look forward to eating at our favorite restaurants.

Nonfiction

THIRTY-FIVE
DEATH AND REBIRTH

Death is a fact of life because our physical bodies are impermanent. They don't last forever. We are subject to change and eventual old age. Some souls live much longer than others. Such individuals have learned to maintain a healthy, physical body for a long period of time.

Death is the transformation of the soul from the Earth plane to the astral plane. The soul travels through a tunnel of light and transcendent colors to the astral plane. We have seven bodies in which we become aware of as we evolve and develop during each incarnation.

We reincarnate in a new physical body each lifetime to continue to learn all we can about the physical plane. Rebirth is the continuation of a soul's experience on the physical plane. We dwell in four lower bodies known as physical, mental, emotional and astral. We have three higher bodies known as the Etheric body, Christ Self and I Am Presence which are on the higher planes.

We are reborn again and again to learn all we can. We have lessons to learn. Once many lessons have been learned we have the opportunity to ascend into the higher astral plane to serve there in our higher bodies. We keep evolving and growing so that we can develop soul mastery. As masters we continue to serve others on the higher planes. So, death and rebirth are continuous experiences.

THE REINCARNATION OF EDGAR CAYCE? written by Wynn Free with David Wilcock describes the life and accomplishments of Edgar Cayce, known as a sleeping prophet of the Twentieth Century. Edgar Cayce was born in 1877 and he died in 1945. Wynn Free and David Wilcox said, "Edgar Cayce left a legacy that has impacted the lives of millions."

Cayce, who died in 1945, announced he would return in 1998. David Wilcock says "he first connected his own dreams with Cayce's trances in November 1997. Edgar Cayce began working with different individuals." Under trance many individuals revealed past lives which were stored in their subconscious mind. Cayce proved that reincarnation exists. Edgar Cayce was recognized in a biography entitled THERE IS A RIVER written by Thomas Sugrue. "His 14,500 documented readings have stood the test of time. He could diagnose the medical condition of anyone regardless of his or her location. He could read someone's past lives and explain how their present circumstances and conditions were influenced by their previous experiences. He could explain the spiritual workings of the universe with facts that no one on the physical Earth could possibly have known. He made startling, accurate predictions of future events, some of which have not yet come to pass."

David Wilcock, who is still living, has come to realize that he was Edgar Cayce in his past life. David Wilcock found out that his astrological signs were similar to Edgar Cayce's astrological signs. David Wilcock looks like Edgar Cayce in physical form. He went to Virginia Beach in Virginia where Edgar Cayce also lived. David discovered more and more about Edgar Cayce's life.

David Wilcock's astrological chart is similar to Edgar Cayce's astrological chart. Both of them had their birth sign in Pisces. The position of the Moon is Taurus. The position of Mercury is Pisces. The position of Venus is Pisces. The position of Mars is Capricorn. The Chinese year is the Ox. The degree of the Moon is 13 degrees. Both astrological charts are the same. David Wilcock's physical appearance and similar interests dovetail with Edgar Cayce. David Wilcock appears to be the reincarnation of Edgar Cayce. He is continuing in the same direction as if he is continuing on with his endeavors and spiritual development and growth.

Fiction

THIRTY-SIX
MEMORABLE AWARENESS

MEMORABLE AWARENESS may occur in our dreams and daydreams. Dreams take us into a colorful, creative state of mind with special effects. Our conscious mind keeps creating images and experiences which are unusual. Our awareness takes place spontaneously. We can remember some dreams which have a deep impact on our conscious minds. Dreams may transform us because of their deep impressions made in our consciousness.

Sharon White often had vivid dreams. She remembered many other dreams when she woke up. She had a memorable dream in which she lived in a magical land of majestic mountains, azure-blue lakes and emerald meadows with golden rods and lupins vividly growing in verdant valleys.

Vivid blue skies, with floating clouds, wisped by over sparkling, rippling water. Magical forests magnified fragrant, misty images of green painted designs sweeping across hillsides near meadows and streams.

Sharon dreamt about a magical kingdom of beautiful women and handsome men who dressed in long, white, gold and purple robes. Their golden hair and crystal blue eyes glowed with beauty and sparkling light. Each person appeared radiant and elegant as they moved gracefully in the meadows and through the mystical forests.

Beams of sun rays shone brightly through the majestic, tall evergreen trees. Sharon walked into the enchanted forest. She saw fairies flying through the trees. The fairies sparkled in their pastel colored gowns with their fluttering, light wings moving quickly like butterflies in the breeze. Sharon was fascinated with the fairies as they fluttered everywhere. Some fairies were dancing in circles. They were singing celestial melodies as they danced and flew around.

Sharon felt blissful in this enchanted, serene abode. She felt like she was in Heaven. Life here was magical and harmonious. Sharon sat down under a large, evergreen pine tree. She watched colorful butterflies flying through this enchanted forest. Colorful flowers were in bloom on the forest floor. Sharon basked in the warm, sun rays beaming through this forest. She wanted to stay here forever to feel at peace.

While Sharon was basking in the sun under a fragrant, protective pine tree she suddenly heard someone's voice nearby. She looked around to find out who was speaking. A golden haired young man, dressed in a white and gold robe, who was wearing golden sandals, appeared before Sharon. She peered at this radiant person. He smiled warmly at her.

Sharon felt completely comfortable when she saw this young man. He spoke first. "Hello. Welcome to our mystical paradise." Sharon looked at this enchanting person. She was amazed at his grace and gentle manner. She smiled back at him. He dazzled with light. He was no ordinary person. Sharon felt loving energy coming from him.

Sharon asked, "Who are you?" The enchanting man replied, "I am Azul. I dwell in this forest. These evergreen trees are my home. They have existed here for thousands of years." Azul asked, "What brings you here? " Sharon answered, "I don't know. I happen to come by. This forest is so magnificent. Have you lived here very long?"

Azul replied, "I have lived here for over a thousand years. Where are you from?" Sharon answered, "I come from Earth." Azul responded, "Earth is in the third dimension. You have come to the fourth dimension." Sharon realized that she wasn't on the Earth's surface. She was on the higher astral plane. She wondered how she got to the fourth dimension.

Azul looked up in the sturdy, evergreen tree Sharon was sitting under. He pointed to some birds in these evergreen trees.

The birds were golden with purple plumes and white beaks. They were chirping in the trees. Their chirping sounds were cheerful and harmonious. Sharon listened attentively to these chirping birds. They sounded almost etheric because of their unusual sounds. Sharon continued to listen to these beautiful birds producing heavenly melodies. These birds were more spiritual and their bird sounds were very special and pure. These fourth dimensional birds produced far more magnificen, musical sounds than birds dwelling in the third dimension.

Sharon was impressed with the fourth dimension because the colors and vibrations were much higher. Harmonious degrees of light colors and geometric designs were visible everywhere. Sharon had her vibration lifted and she was flooded with more light. She was happier than she had ever been in her Earth life.

Azul spoke to Sharon. He said, "Come with me. I will show you something unusual." Sharon was curious. So, she stood up and followed Azul into the forest. As Azul and Sharon walked deep into the forest they came to a golden pathway with sparkling, glittering light. Azul continued walking on this pathway. Sharon followed him. As they walked farther and farther they came to a dimensional pyramid which appeared to be made of a crystal substance.

The crystal pyramid was magical to look at. It appeared to be a geometric palace. Azul took a crystal key and unlocked a triangular door. Azul looked at Sharon and said, "Please enter my crystal domain." Sharon followed Azul into the crystal pyramid. This pyramid structure glowed with white light. At the top of the inside of this crystal pyramid ceiling was a beaming light which blazed around the interior of the pyramid.

The interior of the crystal pyramid had geometric designs and symbols on the crystal, triangular walls. The pyramid floors sparkled with diamond light. In the center of this crystal pyramid an altar stood with diamond and amethyst stones which blazed. A white cross of blazing light beamed with rays of light. Sharon was amazed at this sacred, splendid sight. She felt she was in Heaven

Azul walked over to the central altar. He bowed before it. Sharon stood near this magnificent altar. Azul picked up a white, beaming stone. He touched Sharon's forehead with this white stone. Instantly, Sharon was uplifted by the healing energy and light she experienced from this magnetic stone. Sharon was transformed within all the cells of her physical and astral bodies.

Azul repeated some spiritual chants in an ancient, wisdom language. Sharon witnessed some angels who appeared near the central altar. The angels were dressed in white with glittering wings. They moved above the altar. They circled around Sharon and showered her with pure light. Sharon was sealed with white light around her body. Sharon experienced an ascension into the fourth dimension. She remained in this fourth dimension. She no longer dwelled in the third dimension.

Nonfiction

THIRTY-SEVEN
MOTHS, BUTTERFLIES AND FIREFLIES

Moths, butterflies and fireflies fly around and dwell in gardens, forests and in yards and parks. Moths are usually less colorful than butterflies. Moths seek light near lamps. Moths can fly into closets and eat through clothing. They seek food in houses.

Butterflies have larger wings with a variety of colors. Monarch butterflies are orange, yellow and black. They flutter around flowers, on plants to absorb pollen and dewdrops. Many butterflies fly around in forests. They absorb moisture in the air. They land on branches and leaves to rest.

Fireflies glitter with light during nighttime. Many fireflies send out light as they fly around in the night sky. Fireflies live in warm places. They may live near swamps and in moss-covered trees. They continue to glitter and fly around bringing light. They are interesting to observe especially at night.

Moths, butterflies and fireflies are beautiful and worth observing. They add to nature and are some of the most unusual insects. There are hundreds of different moths and butterflies in the world. Many moths and butterflies are placed in museums in glass cases after they are no longer living. Many people can observe many moths and butterflies with a variety of colors and designs.

Nonfiction

THIRTY-EIGHT
A TRUE STORY ABOUT MY MOTHER

My mother was a special person. She studied Law in New York City while she was in her twenties. She was well educated for a woman who grew up in the 1920s. My mother dressed in stylish 1920s clothes and hats in the 1920s. She wore a 1920s hairstyle.

My mother had a beautiful white and black spotted dog with drooping ears. Her dog responded well to my mother. She walked her dog on long walks daily. Her dog barked at other people who approached my mother. He wanted to protect her from strangers in the street. My mother's dog lived fourteen years.

My mother was very attractive. She went to dances to meet people in her own age group. She had self control. And so she avoided intimacy with the opposite sex. She married a man who was unable to consummate a sexual relationship. She wanted children. Then she met my father at a dance in Los Angeles, California. She began dating my father for a year before they were married in 1928. He drove to Los Angeles on weekends to stay at my mother's home. She was still living with her parents.

My parents were married in Santa Maria, California at a Christian Church. They lived on a ranch near Santa Maria. Within a year they moved to Halcyon, California. They moved into a small house. My father rebuilt this wooden house. He added three bedrooms. He built a large livingroom, kitchen and dining room. My parents had five children.

My mother devoted her life to being a good mother. She gave birth to three boys. In time, she gave birth to twin girls. She was busy day and night taking care of her twins. She fed her twin girls goats' milk which was not pasteurized properly. The twins became very sick. My mother decided not to feed her twins goats' milk which was not pasteurized.

My mother stayed home to raise her children. She was devoted to them. She protected and guided her five children. She encouraged her children to receive a good education which included a higher education. Four out of her five children attended college and received college degrees. She inspired her children to seek the best education possible in order to select worthwhile occupations.

My mother served her family, church and community. She was a generous and giving person. She cared what happened to others. She gave food to people who came to the door. She even served in court on juries to help victims being accused of crimes they didn't commit.

My mother was a hero in my opinion. She was there to be supportive and helpful during crises for all of her children and my father. She was an attentive listener when my brothers played the violin, viola and cello. She listened well when I performed piano solos and vocal solos.

My mother appreciated my achievements and accomplishments in school and in the community. When I earned good grades in school she was positive about my success in school. My academic achievements were important to her.

My mother worked hard for nearly eighteen years at the San Luis Obispo Highway Department. She gave John, David, Roland and me money monthly while we were attending college. Yet, my mother's monthly salary was only $425. Most of the money was given to her children. My mother was unselfish. She could have saved her monthly income for her own living expenses and for vacations. She was willing to give her hard earned income away to help her children receive a higher education.

My mother gathered Christmas gifts all year for our family. She gave each member of our immediate family at least ten presents which were placed under the Christmas tree. Our family opened their Christmas gifts on Christmas Day usually after breakfast. My mother selected very good presents for all of her children and my father. My mother was kind, compassionate, loving and generous. She was a special person.

Nonfiction

THIRTY-NINE
SOLID OBJECTS, LIQUIDS AND GASES

Solid objects exist on Earth. When you touch a wooden table, a wooden chair, lamps, trees, rocks, houses, cars, silverware, plates, cups, glassware and many more objects these objects are made of solid matter.

Solid matter is dense substance which takes a specific form. The molecules have slowed down to become solid. All material things are made of matter.

Liquids move and are formless. Atoms and molecules move quickly in liquids. Water, milk, fruit juice, soft drinks and other beverages such as coffee and tea are liquids. Liquids we drink are poured into glasses, cups and other containers.

Mountains are made of solid rocks and thick soil which are highly raised on Earth. Mountains rise way above sea level. Mountains remain as mountains for a long time. Eventually earthquakes and cataclysms cause mountains to crumble and change shape. However, every mountain is formed with solid matter. Matter can change into different forms and still be solids and liquids.

Liquids can freeze and become ice and snow. Thick ice appears to be solid because the atoms and molecules have slowed down considerably. Ice is solid. Wood and metal are even more solid. Grapefruit and oranges appear completely solid. However, the fruit inside the skin contains liquid.

The Earth is made up of elements, solids, liquids and gases. Liquids evaporate and become vapor. Gases are not solids or liquids. Gases are any mixture of flammable gases used for lighting or cooking. Gases and vapors contain atoms that vibrate much faster than liquids. The slower atoms vibrate the denser and harder objects become. Electricity and light energy vibrate at higher octaves than gases and vapors.

Nonfiction

FORTY
WOOD CARVINGS

W ood carving is a creative, artistic experience. Teakwood, mahogany, redwood and driftwood are used to carve. Many wood carvings are made with quality wood.

Wood carvers use special knives and other cutting tools to carve wood dolls, statuettes and driftwood tables and displays. Driftwood can be polished with a wood glaze.

Eskimos carved wooden totem poles. They created carvings of nature spirits, family members and "gods" on poles. These wood carvings were painted with bright colors. Eskimos placed totem poles in strategic places for wanderers and passer-bys to observe. Wood totem poles also signified religious beliefs that Eskimos focused on. They stood before their wood carvings to worship their gods. They also had wood carvings of evil spirits. They used their totem poles to scare away evil spirits and intruders.

Wood is used to make clocks. Wood spoons are used to hang on the wall as artistic displays. Wooden bowls are shaped and carved to place food in. Wooden plates, forks and ladles are used for dining. Wood ladles can hang on kitchen walls or be placed on tables to place other silver and metal spoons and forks on.

Wooden statuettes and other wood carvings can be displayed on living room, dining room and bedroom shelves as artistic displays. Surfboards were carved out of wood and coated with a protective resin and fiberglass in order to be smooth and polished. Hawaiian kings were the first individuals to go surfing. Sealed wooden surfboards lasted because of the way they were designed.

African tribes designed wooden statues of tribesmen and tribeswomen. They carved wooden dolls and their gods. Africans had shamans, who tried to heal people. Carved masks made of carved wood were worn.

Wood carvings are being created by wood cutters even today. This artistic pursuit is still popular and worthwhile in different places in the world. Many wood carved tables and carefully designed, wood chairs, wood coo coo clocks, driftwood tables, wooden dolls, wooden figurines, wooden jewel boxes and many more wooden carvings are sold in shops and antique stores.

Nonfiction

FORTY-ONE
ABOUT AUDREY HEPBURN

Audrey Hepburn was born in Holland before World War II. She grew up during the war. Food became scarce. Audrey lived with her parents, who struggled to survive during those difficult years. Audrey became a spy for the Hollanders in order to find out what the Nazis were planning to do in Holland. Audrey helped her people to win World War II.

Audrey Hepburn studied ballet when she went to ballet school in Amsterdam in Holland. She studied ballet for several years. She hoped to become a successful ballerina. However, her ballet teacher told her that Audrey was not dancing well enough to become a top ballerina. Audrey felt let down. Yet, she was courteous to her ballet teacher about her comments.

Audrey was spotted by a drama coach one day downtown in a shopping center. The drama coach observed Audrey behaving vivaciously in public. This drama coach decided to talk to Audrey. She told Audrey that she should try out for the part of Gigi on the stage. So, Audrey Hepburn went to the theater to audition for the major role of GIGI. She performed in this stage play and this launched her career as a stage play actress.

Audrey Hepburn was chosen for a major role in ROMAN HOLIDAY. She won an Oscar Academy for her role in ROMAN HOLIDAY. She continued to act in MY FAIR LADY, a Broadway musical. Rex Harrison was the leading man in MY FAIR LADY. Audrey and Rex were very successful in this film.

Audrey Hepburn has acted in other films such as SABRINA with William Holden and Humphrey Bogart. She also acted in CHARADE with Cary Grant and TWO FOR THE ROAD with Albert Finney. Other successful films Audrey performed in are THE NUN'S STORY and DIARY OF ANNE FRANK.

Audrey Hepburn became a superstar. She was quite popular. Audrey Hepburn loved flowers. She cultivated a beautiful garden in her front, side and backyards of her home.

Audrey Hepburn was glad to become a mother of two sons. She was a devoted mother. She loved her two boys and her husband. She lived a life of service and goodwill.

Fiction

FORTY-TWO
PARTY AT THE BEACH

Parties take place on many beaches. People like to get together to celebrate on beaches. They bring food and build fires to cook wieners and marshmallows. Blankets and towels are placed on the warm sand for people to sit on and lay down to bask in the sun.

Cheryl Mitchell liked to go to the beach in Venice, California. She planned a party at this beach. She invited her friends to come to the beach on Saturday at 3 p.m. for a beach party. Cheryl planned to bring hot dogs, mustard, catsup, relish, pickles, potato salad, lettuce, tomatoes, potato chips, cookies, cake, cold drinks and cut vegetables such as carrots, green peppers and cucumbers. Cheryl also provided paper plates, napkins, plastic cups and plastic silverware.

On Saturday Cheryl packed all the picnic food and utensils in her car. She headed to Venice Beach. When she got there she unpacked all of the food and utensils onto the white, sandy beach. The beach sand was warm under her bare feet. Cheryl placed blankets and towels on the beach.

Cheryl waited for her friends to arrive for the beach party. While she waited she dug a hole and placed fire wood in the hole. She folded scraps of paper and put them over the fire wood. She lit the paper. The fire began to burn. Cheryl began cooking wieners on long sticks over the burning fire.

Cheryl's friends arrived one by one at the beach dressed in bathing suits and casual clothing. Each of Cheryl's friends brought folding, beach chairs to sit in.

After everyone arrived Cheryl announced that it was time to eat. Each person served himself or herself to the prepared party food. There were plenty of wieners that had been roasted over the fire. Everyone took hot dog buns and spread catsup, mustard and relish on them. Then they put a wiener in each bun. They served themselves potato salad, cut veggies and potato chips. Sliced cake was available to select along with homemade, oatmeal cookies. Cold drinks and hot coffee were served by Cheryl.

After everyone ate their food a volleyball net was set up. Two teams played volleyball. They hit the volleyball back and forth over the net. When the ball fell or went outside the designated volleyball court the other team earned volleyball points. They kept playing until a team won.

The ocean waves were crashing to shore. Cheryl's friends walked in the wet sand and ocean to enjoy the rhythm of the sea. They felt the warm sun on their skin. Some of them went swimming in the ocean. Waves rolled over them. Their hair and whole bodies were covered with ocean water.

Later, some of Cheryl's friends played guitars on the beach near the shimmering fire. Everyone sang folk songs and other songs. They were having a good time. Some of them danced to the guitar music.

The beach party lasted for hours. Around 9:15 p.m. it was dark on the beach. Everyone watched the sunset first. Then they watched the Moon come up. It appeared very large over the ocean. The stars came out and glittered. The Big Dipper, the Little Dipper, the North Star, Venus and Jupiter were visible. The night sky was beautiful.

Once the party was over everyone helped to clean up. When the remaining food and utensils were gathered and placed in Cheryl's car everyone thanked Cheryl for inviting them to the beach party. Cheryl was glad they had a good time. She planned to have another beach party in the near future.

Nonfiction

FORTY-THREE
MY FAVORITE MOVIES

 $\mathbf{M}$ any movies have been produced through the years since the 1920s. I have seen hundreds of films since I was a child and into an adult. As a child my favorite movies were THE WIZARD OF OZ with Judy Garland, CINDERELLA, THE JUNGLE BOOK, ADVENTURES OF TARZAN, ROY ROGERS AND DALE EVANS and BAMBI. These films were children's classics. The main characters were my childhood heroes because of their character roles and images. I was impressionable as a child. The characters expressed role models in these films.

As an adult my favorite movies are THE GREATEST STORY EVER TOLD which is about the mission of Jesus Christ. BRIGADOON is a Scottish musical with Cyd Cyrise and Gene Kelly. MY FAIR LADY is a musical in London, England starring Audrey Hepburn and Rex Harrison.. THE LIFE OF GANDHI was a very impressive film about Mahatma Gandhi, a great leader of India who used nonviolent, political methods to resolve political problems and issues in India during the 1930s and 1940s.

DEEP IN MY HEART is a film about the musical career of Sigmund Romberg. He produced many Broadway musicals which were magnificent such as MAYTIME, JAZZ A DO and STUDENT PRINCE, etc.

Other favorite films I have enjoyed are ROMAN HOLIDAY with Audrey Hepburn and Gregory Peck which is about the adventures of a princess who escaped from her role as a princess for a night and day. THE UNSINKABLE MOLLY BROWN with Debbie Reynolds and Harvey Presnel was about Molly Brown's life in Colorado. I enjoyed TAMMY which was produced in the 1950s with Debbie Reynolds. NATIONAL VELVET with Elizabeth Taylor and Mickie Rooney was about a 12 year old English girl who won a horse race in the English Derby. BAND WAGON is another musical with stars such as Fred Astaire, Cyd Cyrise and others who performed Broadway songs and perform dynamic excerpts. THE MUSIC MAN, starring Shirley Jones and Robert Preston, is another dynamic musical which was produced in Iowa. It is about a salesman who wished he could be a real band leader.

My favorite movies are films which have worthwhile stories and plots. The characters have values and convictions in these stimulating movies. Many of my favorite movies have become classics which other people also appreciate. These classics are shown on television today so many people can enjoy these films.

Nonfiction

FORTY-FOUR
WHY ACTORS AND ACTRESSES SUCCEED

Superstars become famous because of their ability to act on the stage and in films. Super stars become very well known and they star in main roles in many movies.

Some super stars are Elizabeth Taylor, James Stuart, Debbie Reynolds, Richard Burton, Robert Taylor, Robert Redford, Charleston Heston, Jean Simmons, Michelle Pheiffer, Michael Landon, Debra Kerr, Marilyn Monroe, Gary Cooper, Grace Kelley, Peter Lawford, Paul Newman, Spencer Tracy, Katherine Hepburn, Audrey Hepburn, Gregory Peck, Cary Grant, Humphrey Bogart, Lawrence Oliviea, Kirk Douglas, Dorothy McGuire, Frank Sinatra, Doris Day, Rod Taylor, Rock Hudson, Judy Garland, Gene Kelley, Fred Astaire, John Wayne, Burt Reynolds, Henry Fonda, Peter Fonda, Jane Fonda, Julie Christie, Brad Pitt, Mel Gibson, Cameron Diaz, Clint Eastwood, etc.

These super stars have performed in many movies over the years. They have become popular because they have a certain unique style of acting which has made them known. They dress a certain way and have interesting hairstyles. They have specific talents which make them stand out. They have become super stars because they have developed a reputation as very successful actors and actresses.

Nonfiction

FORTY-FIVE
THE WHITE HOUSE IN WASHINGTON D.C.

The White House in Washington D.C. is the most beautiful building in the world. The President of the United States lives in the White House with his immediate family. His wife and children live there with him.

The White House was built in 1800. John Adams and his wife, Abigail were the first to move in when John Adams became the second President of America. The White House was still being built and renovated. Abigail hung laundry up in the East Wing of the White House.

As each President moved into the White House changes were made. A larger bathtub was put in the President's bathroom when Harrison was President. Franklin Roosevelt added an indoor swimming pool. Jackie Kennedy redecorated many rooms in the White House by having them repainted. New curtains were added. More paintings and new furniture replaced older, less attractive furnishings. Richard Nixon added a pool room. The Oval Office was redecorated several times. New carpets were installed. The President's desk stands out in the Oval Office. John F. Kennedy, Junior crawled under the President's desk when he was a child.

In the White House there are many rooms. There are the East Room and State Dining Room, which are the largest rooms in the White House. The Red Room, Blue Room and Green Room are painted according to their designated colors. These rooms look elegant. Large dinners are served in the State Dining room. There are many circular tables decorated with colorful table cloths, very elegant plates, cups, saucers and glasses. Gold silverware is used with fancy napkins. The State dining room is decorated with beautiful flowers. Many dinners are served here.

Political leaders from around the world are invited to the White House. They attend State Room dinners which are elaborately prepared by many cooks and served by the White House Staff. Each dinner is especially prepared to please visitors who come to the White House.

The East Room had to be restored in the 1940s when a piano leg fell through the floor. The Oval Office is in another, large building. A guard stands outside the Oval Office. This room was designed in an oval shape so the President could see everyone easier who entered the Oval Office.

There are special, living quarters where the President and his family live full time. The living quarters are nicely decorated. Each President and his family add their own personal touch to the living area. There are beautiful gardens surrounding the White House.

There are special, living quarters where the President and his family live full time. The living quarters are nicely decorated. Each President and his family added their own personal tough to the living area. There are beautiful gardens surrounding the White House. 18 acres of land are covered with many trees, magnificent flowers and verdant-green lawns. The President and his family can take walks around the grounds.

George Washington, the first President of America, never lived in the White House. He lived at Mount Vernon and in New York City. He governed America from a Washington's Headquarters in New York City.

The White House is kept very clean and neat. It is the only governmental home to be open to the public to tour through to see what this magnificent American home looks like. There are historical, American paintings, statues, mirrors and large photographs of the American presidents displayed in different rooms in the White House so visitors can appreciate American, historical reminders.

Many people are invited to musical presentations in the East Room. Different well known vocal soloists such as Frank Sinatra, Marian Anderson, Nat King Cole, Bing Crosby and others have performed in the East Room at the White House.

Through careful investigation some reports indicate that there is a secret White House deep below Mount Weather in West Virginia. It can be reached by traveling on an underground bullet train. There is fresh water and electric lighting. This secret place includes malls, homes and gardens. A secret underground Pentagon also exists. This secret governmental place was built in the 1950s-1960s. Presidents, cabinets, military leaders, congressional leaders, national department directors and other important officials have access to this secret underground community. If an atomic attack, meteor, comet or other natural disaster destroys the surface of the United States these leaders a place to escape. Government offices, homes, businesses and facilities with computers, generators, alternative energy systems, supermarkets and other essential facilities exist underground. It is reported they have a fifty year supply of food, water, energy and infrastructure. This secret, underground community is designed to insure that the U.S. government can function efficiently if its outer structures and infrastructure are destroyed. A secret, back up, emergency, alternative government is always underground to take over the U.S.A. if leaders on the surface are killed. Massive, underground libraries and computer files are stored with all necessary knowledge to continue an advanced civilization and technology.

Millions of people have come to see the White House in Washington D.C. through the years since it has become a public place to tour through. At one time it was strongly suggested that the White House be moved inland away from the ocean. However, this plan was abandoned. The White House is protected by a metal, protective fence to keep intruders out after visiting time. Buildings on the grounds are used for governmental events and activities. The White House is considered to be the most beautiful building in the world.

Nonfiction

FORTY-SIX
LISTENING TO MUSIC

When you wake up in the morning it is relaxing to listen to music. There is an Easy Listening channel on television. Many composers and musicians perform instrumental music. Such musicians are Roger Williams who plays the piano and has composed and performed with an orchestra. He has played many popular, piano pieces with background instrumentalists. He began playing at an early age.

Other well known musicians, who also play solo instruments, are Lawrence Welk, Johnny Douglas, Percy Faith, Lloyd Cramer, Akkar Blk, Paul Murial, Johnny Mercer, Ronnie Aldrich, Michael Farmon, Beegie Adair, Richard Clayderman, Henry Mancini, Montovani, Andre Kostelanetz, John Fox, Pete Fountain, Chet Atkins and more. Each of these musicians has devoted their lives to their careers as performers. Their music is pleasant to listen to.

Classical music is worth listening to as well. Classical composers are Mozart, Beethoven, Mendelsohn, Debussy, Hayden, Weber, Chopin, Bach, Shubert, Bartok, Grieg, Lizyt, Rossini, Shumann, Tchaikovsky, Puccini and Wagner. Each of these composers created unique compositions for many people to enjoy and appreciate.

Classical music is well developed with different instruments being played in a beautiful manner. Many stimulating compositions have been written. If you listen to preludes, sonatas, interludes and polonaises these forms of music uplift you because of their melodic quality. Melodic music helps us feel better because it is harmonious and in tune with nature and God.

Avoid listening to harsh, disharmonious music because this type of music is not in tune with nature. Disharmonious music is not healthy to listen to. This kind of music can affect your nervous system in the wrong way.

It is best to select relaxing, harmonious music which is healing to the emotional and mental body. Start your day with positive thoughts and prayers. Then listen to uplifting music so you will feel better during the day.

In the 1980s to 1990s hundreds of albums of instrumental New Age Music were produced and sold. Many of these recordings used certain, specific, tonal frequencies designed to heal the body, balance brain waves, reduce stress, improve emotions, expand consciousness, balance the chakras, and enhance meditation. A couple of the best albums were MUSIC TO DISAPPEAR IN by Raphael and MUSIC FROM THE PLEIADES by Gerald Jay Markoe. However, there are many more of these tapes and CDs by other composers, including newer compositions in the 21st Century. Most New Age Music has been sold in metaphysical stores.

It was proven that this type of music also helped plants to grow faster, healthier and produce bigger and better fruit and vegetables. Disharmonious music was observed to cause plants to wither and die faster.

Some of the most popular classical music has been Spanish, flamenco guitar music by Sabicas, Jose Feliciano and other complex, innovative composers. Furthermore, some great bands known mostly for rock and blues have also composed some great classical music with full orchestras and beautiful harmonies. On the leading edge is the Moody Blues. The instrumental aspects of some Beatles ballads, has also become popular, instrumental classics heard on the classical music TV channel. However, most of the best composed classical, music "originals" of the past two decades has been by New Age bands.

Fiction

FORTTY-SEVEN
VICTORIES AND DEFEATS

We experience victories and defeats in life. When we are uplifted, happy and have positive experiences we feel victorious. When we felt let down, despondent and unhappy we may feel defeated.

Syvania Jenson felt wonderful when she was chosen to act in a major role in a high school play. She rehearsed after school several days a week to prepare for the stage play to be presented in the high school gym. Syvania was a very good actress on the stage. She possessed charm, charisma and a natural ability to act.

Many people attended the school stage play entitled UNTAMED LANDSCAPE. Sylvania was very successful in her major role in this play. She felt elated and victorious as an actress. Syvania was successful in school. She was popular and healthy. Her life was going along smoothly. She was a happy person because she was successful in everything she did.

Syvania liked to go skiing as a hobby. She had been skiing for several years. Syvania went skiing on the weekends up in the Sun Valley Ski Resort. She only lived approximately one hundred miles south of the Sun Valley Ski Resort in Idaho.

One day when Syvania was skiing on the ski slope she went on her skis down the steep ski slopes. She was moving swiftly down a steep slope. At first she skied smoothly down the snowy slope.

Suddenly Syvania hit a softer part of the slope. Her skis began to tip to an awkward position. Syvania turned over quickly and she lost control and went tumbling down very swiftly. She felt a very sharp, piercing pain in her legs and back as she rolled over and over. She landed in a snowy spot finally after rolling over and over.

Syvania finally stopped moving. She felt severe pain in her body as she laid helpless in the snow. As she laid in the snow she felt very helpless when she tried to move to get up. She was unable to get up. Syvania remained helpless in the cold snow unable to pull herself up. She had never felt this way before. She was forced to stay helpless and alone.

It took at least fifteen minutes before someone came to rescue Syvania. Syvania had to be picked up and be taken to the Emergency Ward at the closest hospital. She had two broken legs and her spine had been effected by the fall.

Syvania was taken into the Emergency Ward on a stretcher from the ambulance which had come to rescue her. She was completely helpless which was a shock to her emotionally and psychologically. Sylvania had never been helpless like this before. She was hurting badly from her sudden, severe fall. A nurse took her vital signs. Then a doctor in the Emergency Room examined her closely.

The doctor told Sylvania that both of her legs were broken and that her spine had been injured.. Sylvania felt defeated because of this unpleasant news. She realized that she would not be able to walk and be independent for some time. She continued to lie in bed because she was unable to walk. She tried not to feel defeated. However, she kept thinking about her severe, physical set back. She became depressed more and more. Her future seemed very dim and meaningless.

Syvania watched television to pass the time away. She became despondent and bored because she was unable to move around freely as she once was able to move. She began to try different things to do while she was in bed. She learned to knit once she was able to sit up in bed. This helped her to preoccupy her time. She looked out the window at the view of a garden and mountain in the distance. Syvania read books to stimulate her mind and imagination. She began to learn more and more as she read worthwhile books. Syvania tried to exercise her broken legs as they were healing.

After months of healing Syvania was able to use a wheelchair to sit in to move around in. She still felt despondent and had periods of depression. She kept occupied however with different things to do. Syvania began to exercise a little each day. Finally her legs began to heal. She hoped to be able to walk again.

Gradually, Syvania regained strength in her legs. She began to walk again. As she learned she began to feel better physically and emotionallywith more balance. She was regaining her strength day by day. Within four months her legs were nearly well. Syvania went to physical therapy to heal her injured spine. In time, Syvania was able to walk with a walker.

Syvania decided she would never go skiing again. She didn't want to risk being in an accident on skis again. She began to think more positive. She felt happy again.

Nonfiction

FORTY-EIGHT
ATTACHMENT TO RESULTS

Quite often we are attached to results. We want others to praise us for our accomplishments. When we work hard we want to be appreciated for our work. We want other people to notice our talents and abilities.

Some people become entertainers and performers. They play a musical instrument or become a vocal soloist. Some people become actors and actresses; while others become artists or poets. These talented people want to be successful and recognized for their achievements.

Rembrandt became a well known, painter-artist in Holland in the 17th Century. He painted many portraits of people living in Amsterdam and in Holland's countryside. He chose poor people to paint. He made them look like wealthy people. Rembrandt hoped to become a famous artist. Rembrandt did not make much money as an artist during his lifetime. In fact, he died as a poor man. He kept on painting until the end of his life. He was attached to making a name as an artist. Years after his death, Rembrandt's paintings became very valuable. His paintings were displayed at many historical museums in Europe and America.

Liberace began performing in Milwaukee, Wisconsin in public. He enjoyed performing publicly. He appreciated applause and cheers from audiences. He wanted to become well known and famous as a pianist. In time, Liberace became famous when he performed on The Liberace Show in Hollywood, California. Liberace thanked his audiences for clapping graciously. He was attached to results because he wanted to be famous and wealthy. He fulfilled his wishes by becoming famous and wealthy.

Liberace spent money on luxurious clothes, expensive houses and cars. He installed large swimming pools at several homes. Liberace enjoyed living in luxury and elegance as a regular high class lifestyle. Liberace was strongly attached to being successful as a top musician.

The Beatles who became known in Liverpool, England performed while they were teenagers. They became popular after they performed on The Ed Sullivan Show. They toured around the world performing as a quartet. They dressed up in fancy outfits. They wanted to become well known and famous. They also wanted to be the most popular performers in the world. They were attached to results as musicians. The Beatles composed a variety of songs such as THE YELLOW SUBMARINE, YESTERDAY and THE LONG AND WINDING ROAD, etc., to seek fame and fortune. They succeeded in becoming on the top of the music charts on the radio and television.

Many famous musicians, actors and actresses become very attached to results. They want to become well known, famous and wealthy in their careers. They are ambitious and hard working to become successful and popular in order to achieve fame and fortune.

Fiction

FORTY-NINE
THE LARGE BALLOON

Balloons are blown up with air. They are able to move up into the sky. Balloons are lifted by wind and breezes. There are small and large balloons. They bounce around and float in the air. There are many different colors such as red, blue, green, yellow, orange, purple, turquoise, pink and more used to color balloons.

Julie McIntosh enjoyed blowing up rubber balloons. She tied a knot in each balloon she blew up. Then she tied a string on the knot of each balloon. Julie put a group of balloons tied to strings and held the strings of balloons in the air to display them to anyone walking by. The seven balloons swayed in the breeze above Julie's head.

Balloons were sold at shops downtown. Julie decided to buy a large, purple, rubber balloon. Once she purchased this large balloon she took it out into a nearby field. She attached a long string to it and let it float in the sky. This large, purple balloon could be seen for miles away.

People traveled in their cars towards the large, purple balloon in order to look at it up close. They stood out in the open field to enjoy this balloon floating in the sky. Little children came over to Julie, who was holding the long string attached to this large balloon. They had fun watching this balloon move in the air.

Suddenly, a very strong wind came across the sky. Julie accidentally let go of the long string. The large balloon began floating away in the sky. It rose higher and higher and it moved across the sky. It kept drifting farther away. The crowd in the field was disappointed that the large, purple balloon was disappearing.

Julie got in her car and tried to follow the large balloon. It kept moving farther away. It finally disappeared from sight, high in the sky. Julie felt concerned that she had lost her large, purple balloon. She decided to go back to the store to purchase another large balloon. She would be more careful this time so she wouldn't lose her new, large, green balloon.

Fiction

FIFTY
THE VACATION

Ralph and William Cox had vacation time coming. They planned to take their vacation at the same time so they could be together while they enjoyed their free time. Ralph and Wilma had saved their money so they could take a worthwhile vacation.

Wilma and Ralph discussed how they would enjoy their vacation for two weeks. They studied a U.S. map. They planned to travel in their Honda four door car. Their Honda Deluxe was a sturdy, comfortable car to travel in.

Ralph and Wilma decided to travel to the Great Lakes and to Niagara Falls. They would have to travel at least one thousand miles northeast before they came to the Great Lakes. They lived in Oklahoma City, Oklahoma. The Coxes packed their car with camping equipment and baskets of food such as sandwiches, cut vegetables and fruit. They also brought cookies and muffins along to munch on as snacks.

Wilma and Ralph began their vacation the next morning. Ralph drove their car first on a freeway northeast toward the Great Lakes. They saw forests of evergreen trees. Pine and spruce trees were fragrant as they drove by. They stopped along the roadside near a grove of avocado trees to eat their lunch. Wilma took some tuna sandwiches and cut carrots and green peppers out of a basket. She handed Ralph a tuna sandwich and cut vegetables to eat. She also took a tuna sandwich out of the basket for herself.

Ralph and Wilma sat under avocado trees in the shade to eat their lunch. They sipped ice tea which Wilma poured into two glasses from a thermos container. It was a pleasant, late, spring day. Ralph and Wilma finished their sandwiches and vegetables. They ate an apple for dessert.

After lunch Ralph and Wilma walked through the avocado grove to exercise their legs. Avocados were growing on the trees. Wilma and Ralph picked some avocados to take with them. They would eat these avocados later on with other meals. They walked back to their car with the avocados. They continued their journey northeast.

Ralph continued to drive along the two-way road. They passed a beautiful, azure-blue lake. The sun gleamed on the lake. The glittering sunlight sparkled on this lake. Ralph drove near this lake for several miles. Wilma and Ralph enjoyed the splendid beauty of this lake.

It became dark by late afternoon. The moon came out and moved across the clear, night sky. Stars glittered and twinkled in the night sky. Ralph and Wilma knew it was time to find a camping place for the night. They came to a cluster of trees and decided to bed down for the night under the stars. Ralph parked the car near the trees away from the road. Ralph and Wilma took their bedrolls out of the car. They placed a canvas on the ground under the trees. The bedrolls were put on the canvas.

Ralph and Wilma brought a basket of food out of the car to eat for dinner. Wilma took some baked chicken, potato salad and tomatoes out of the basket. Wilma sliced the tomatoes plus some avocados for them to eat with their chicken and potato salad. They drank more tea with their dinner.

Wilma and Ralph gazed at the stars in the sky. They noticed Polaris, the North Star. They saw Mars, the red planet and Venus. The full moon shone brightly in the night sky. They heard owls hooting nearby. After gazing at the night sky, Ralph and Wilma decided to go to bed early. They planned to get up early to continue their journey.

During the night the owls continued to hoot. Squirrels scurried around in the nearby trees. They climbed up the trunks of trees. Several deer appeared in the distance. They nibbled on grass, leaves and tree moss. Wilma and Ralph enjoyed observing owls, squirrels and deer nearby. They felt close to nature as they relaxed under the cluster of trees. They got into their bedrolls. The night air was warm enough. Ralph and Wilma went to sleep.

The next morning Wilma and Ralph woke up early when the sun was rising over the horizon. They saw more squirrels scurrying around in nearby trees. They were gathering pine cones to take to their tree nests. Some wild hares were scampering by. They nibbled grass and roots on the ground. Robins and sparrows were chirping in the trees. Some birds flew back and forth from the ground to the tree branches where they perched to look around. Some birds were searching for seeds on the ground.

Wilma and Ralph ate some fruit and bread for breakfast. They rolled up their bedrolls and folded the canvas. They put the bedrolls and canvas back in their car. Wilma decided to drive. They stepped into their car and Wilma drove the car back on the road and headed northeast. The Coxes continued their journey towards the Great Lakes. Along the road they passed meadows, streams and mountains which were visible from the road.

The next day Ralph and Wilma came to Lake Michigan. This lake is enormous and beautiful. The Coxes drove near this lake. They came to Detroit, Michigan. Wilma and Ralph were hungry because they had been traveling for hours. So, they stopped at a resort and enjoyed a gourmet, buffet luncheon with all the trimmings. They sat near a large window and enjoyed a marvelous view of the lake while they enjoyed their meal.

After lunch Ralph and Wilma continued driving east through Michigan. They passed many evergreen trees and continued to Lake Erie. They stopped at the Erie Canal which is known for boats which were pulled by mules one hundred fifty years ago. Ralph and Wilma walked near the famous canal. They continued to Buffalo, New York. They drove near Lake Erie all the way to Buffalo. They ate dinner at a cozy café near the shore of Lake Erie. They ordered salmon with red baked potatoes and green salad. For dessert they had custard pudding with whipped cream. Ralph ordered white wine. Wilma and Ralph gazed at Lake Erie as they sipped their wine. They were relaxing as they enjoyed the ambiance and magnificent view of this majestic lake. A full moon beamed over the lake and reflected into the deep blue water.

The next day after spending the night at an inn near Lake Erie Ralph and Wilma headed for Niagara Falls. They drove through Cleveland, Ohio along Lake Erie to Buffalo, New York. It took them more than half a day to reach Buffalo where they stayed overnight in a hotel. They were eager to go to the Niagara Falls to see many waterfalls merging together from different rivers. Niagara Falls is the largest waterfall in the world. Many couples come to Niagara Falls to enjoy their honeymoons.

Ralph and Wilma got up early the next morning. They drove to Niagara Falls. When they approached the Niagara Falls they were amazed at how much water was falling quickly over the Falls. Tons of water flow over Niagara Falls 24 hours a day. Ralph and Wilma parked their car near the edge of the Niagara Falls. They stepped out of their car to observe these spectacular Falls. They saw how many rivers merged together and flowed into the enormous river.

Ralph and Wilma witnessed rainbows in the mist which sprayed in the air at Niagara Falls. Beautiful, rainbow colors looked especially magnificent to view. Ralph and Wilma were fascinated at this unusual sight. They went into the city of Niagara Falls to locate a motel so they could stay overnight.

Once the Coxes found a motel they put their belongings into their motel room. They walked downtown Niagara Falls City to look around at the shops and galleries. They ate at an outdoor restaurant at a terraced garden that night. Colorful, manmade colors were reflected over the Niagara Falls. There were red, green, purple and yellow lights glowing in the falling water. This splendid panoramic sight was so beautiful to observe.

Ralph and Wilma were so glad that they had come to Niagara Falls to see this extraordinary sight. This experience topped their vacation because this was the first time they had seen the Niagara Falls in person

Nonfiction

FIFTY-ONE
LIVING ON A RAFT

Living on a raft can be a challenge because it is a limited space. A raft is made of wood logs and slabs of wood. Some rafts have a sail while other rafts just float in moving water such as rivers, streams and oceans. Modern rafts are made of thick, inflated rubber. Rubber rafts can be stored in airplanes and ships. When they are needed these rubber rafts are blown up with air and placed in rivers or oceans for passengers to navigate in.

If an airplane lands in the ocean, rafts are dropped down in the ocean which automatically inflate and then are ready to use. These rafts are used during emergencies. Ships store rafts which also are used in case the ship is sinking.

What would it be like to live on a raft? Mark Twain wrote about Tom Sawyer and Huckleberry Finn who traveled down the Mississippi River on a wooden raft. Some wooden rafts have a small room with a roof. If it rained passengers can stay inside the enclosed section on the raft. This protective shelter may be used to store supplies and food.

Living on a raft can be an adventure because a person can travel from one place to another. The raft may be smaller than a ship or large boat. Passengers can walk in large rafts. These rafts are controlled by using poles to push these rafts in the direction the passengers want to travel. Too many passengers may cause the raft to sink. Be sure not to have too many passengers on a raft if you want to keep your raft afloat. Bring enough supplies and food for your journey on your raft.

It is important to take care of a raft so it can function properly. A punctured raft is useless. Holes causing leaks in a wooden raft can cause the raft to sink and become useless. Be ready to repair your rubber or wooden raft. Holes can be repaired in both types of rafts if you keep tools which can be used to repair holes and leaks.

Ancient civilizations navigated in rafts across the oceans and across long rivers to travel to distant places. Ancient Polynesians traveled in small boat-like rafts. Ancient Egyptians traveled in large, raft-like boats down the Nile River and to other countries. These ancient navigators learned to live in a limited space. Paddles were used to move their rafts.

Nonfiction

FIFTY-TWO
MIDDLE AGE CHALLENGES

Middle age begins at 45 and continues until 55. Age 56 and above is the beginning of old age. Many people live to be 65 and above. At least 30% of our world's population live to be 80. Around 10% live to be 85 to 90. 5% live to be 95 to 97. About 1% live to be 100 years old.

Middle aged people from 45 to 55 go through emotional and physical changes which affect their attitudes and behavior. Middle aged people may feel insecure and unattractive because they look older and possibly out of physical shape.

Some middle aged people attend therapy groups in order to express their feelings and experiences during middle age. Some middle aged people have stated that they feel rejected and lonely because they are getting older and less capable of maintaining a meaningful relationship with the opposite sex.

When middle aged people are frustrated and feel insecure they may become vulnerable. They want to be desirable and well liked despite their middle aged physical problems. Some middle aged individuals reach sexual climaxes especially at this time of life because they want to please the opposite sex. They want to be happy and sexually fulfilled as well as socially desirable.

Middle aged individuals begin to acquire gray hair. They may begin to experience wrinkles. Men tend to develop fat around their mid ribs and abdomens. Their teeth may begin to deteriorate. They don't appear as handsome as they once were. Men go through middle age crises. They may attempt to have affairs with different women to fulfill their desire to remain desirable and emotionally fulfilled.

Middle aged women try to look glamorous. They may change their hair color. They use cosmetic methods to make their faces look younger. They wear youthful clothes as well as make-up on their faces. Middle aged women want to be desirable to the opposite sex. They want to be attractive and well liked. They want to impress others with their new hairstyles and new clothes. They go to the dentist to improve their teeth. Healthy front teeth help women look attractive.

Some middle aged women and men look much younger than they really are. They feel good when they think they are attractive and desirable.

Nonfiction

FIFTY-THREE
USES OF BATTERIES

Batteries are charged with stored electricity. There are many kinds of batteries. For instance, there are car batteries with positive and negative electric energy which charges the car battery so a car can function properly.

Other batteries are much smaller. Batteries are metal components with stored electricity to use to light flashlights, to charge blow hair dryers, electric shavers, cell phones, car lights, use in television monitors to turn televisions on and off. Monitors for television are used to change channels as well. Batteries may be inserted in portable radios, car radios, inside small televisions, in movable cooking equipment for camping and traveling purposes.

Some portable, lap top computers are operated with computer batteries. Portable televisions may be operated with batteries.

Batteries have been used for over 75 years to operate household appliances, mechanical devices and other items. Batteries are handy and useful especially when household items can not be plugged in the wall. These devices can be used with batteries in place of electricity from wall outlets.

Batteries will continue to be used in home appliances and for traveling purposes. Stored, electrical energy is handy and useful for emergencies as well. Electric generators in hotels and other buildings are operated with large batteries when regular electric lighting is not available. Electric battery-run generators are necessary so business establishments may continue to function and keep businesses continuing when regular, electric lights are off.

Nonfiction

FIFTY-FOUR
CAGED BIRDS

P eople acquire birds for pets. The birds are purchased at pet stores and other places. Birds are caged in order to keep them from flying away.

Cages for birds are different sizes. Birds in zoos usually have larger cages. They may dwell in aviaries with other birds. Small bird cages are used indoors for parakeets, parrots toucans and cockadoos. Larger cages outdoors are used for pigeons, doves, peacocks, quails, etc.

Pieces of wood are made into perches and artificial branches. Bird seed is put inside bird cages. Water containers provide necessary water for caged birds. Birds exist in the same cages. They need companionship with other birds.

Birds are kept in cages for traveling purposes. The caged birds are kept in the storage area of airplanes and trains.

Birds have to learn to adapt to dwelling in cages and aviaries. The temperature should be kept warm enough so caged birds will not freeze to death. They need to be fed at least twice a day to have enough to eat and drink. Their cages need to be cleaned out regularly to keep the cages clean and attractive. Cages generally are washed out to dissolve odors. Birds need to have a clean, attractive environment to dwell in.

MARVELOUS REFLECTIONS

Owners of caged birds usually cover the cages at night time so their caged birds will not be distracted during the night. Birds tend to quiet down at night if their cages are covered up. Birds generally live longer if they are properly cared for.

Nonfiction

FIFTY-FIVE
THE OLDEST PERSON

The oldest person in the world has lived longer than anyone else because he or she has maintained a healthy body over many years. This person has good circulation, breaths well and has good teeth and eyes in order to function effectively.

The oldest person in the world properly exercised and ate organic foods such as raw fruit and vegetables and natural grains produced into homemade bread. He or she drank pure water without pollution.

The oldest person in the world lives in a healthy environment with fresh, clean air and naturally, healthy foods. He or she most likely maintains emotional and mental balance.

A newspaper article stated that a man, who was a vegan, lived to be 156. He lived in the Himalayan Mountains. The air is clean and pure in the Himalayan Mountains. He may have gone hiking in the mountains to strengthen his body.

The oldest man probably had a purpose for his life. He may have fulfilled his goal to maintain good health. He continued to maintain his good health until his death.

We can learn from individuals who live long lives. We can investigate how they lived. Their lifestyle may give us clues why they lived longer than other people. Where did they live? What kind of environment were they exposed to? What kind of food did they eat? How often did they exercise? Did they sleep well and get enough rest? Did they have a strong reason to live? The answers to these questions will help us find out why they lived much longer lives.

Nonfiction

FIFTY-SIX
MY BEST FRIEND

My best friend would be someone I can trust, respect and feel close to. I would be able to communicate well and freely about a wide variety of topics and issues. I can trust that my best friend will not gossip about me. He or she is confidential about my personal life.

My best friend will not try to harm me. He or she appreciates me and accepts me as I am. I can feel comfortable and relaxed around my best friend. I don't have to pretend to act like someone else. I can tell this person my deepest thoughts and express my genuine feelings about life.

My best friend is someone who I can rely and depend on to be supportive and helpful. My best friend will come to my rescue during a crisis. My best friend believes in me and understands my philosophy of life.

My best friend supports my goals and values year by year. He or she cares what happens to me. I can relate especially well with my best friend. I can have a long term friendship with my best friend. Long term friendships are very worthwhile. I am able to witness how my best friend lives, responds and thinks over a long period of time. I am grateful to have a best friend.

Nonfiction

FIFTY-SEVEN
TIMELY EVENTS

We look forward to timely events such as specific holidays, festivals, parades, family celebrations, marriage ceremonies, church activities and planned vacations. These timely events are important and worthwhile. We look forward to special occasions because they bring us happiness. We become overjoyed when we attend birthday parties, wedding receptions, baby showers and wedding showers. Parties held at friends' homes are exciting and usually eventful.

Mardi Gras is a big, planned event which takes place once a year for a week or two in Rio De Janeiro in South America. Mardi Gras also takes place in New Orleans in Louisiana. Everyone dresses up in elaborate costumes. Many participants walk in parades to show off their costumes. Many people save a lot of money to pay for their costumes.

Another timely event is the Gay 90s Festival in September every year in Arroyo Grande, California. A parade is organized with floats, bands and people in a variety of costumes to display 1890s costumes. Booths are set up with a variety of things to purchase plus fast food such as hot dogs, hamburgers, cotton candy, icecream, soft drinks, coffee, pie and cake, etc.

The Pismo Clam Festival is held once a year in Pismo Beach, California. Pismo Beach's famous clam chowder is served. Fish and chips are also served. People witness a parade. Pismo Beach is known for its many clams. It is a tourist town.

Santa Maria has a rodeo once a year. There is a parade with horsemen and horsewomen who dress up in cowboy outfits. Bands play in parades. A barbecue is held after the parade. A rodeo, where cattle such as bulls and calves are roped by different cowboys, takes place. Bulls are challenged with red scarves.

Thanksgiving is a planned event every year to celebrate abundance and thanksgiving for enough food during early America. Christmas is celebrated in December every year in honor of the birth of Jesus Christ. Christmas trees are decorated. Christmas carols are sung during this festive time. Christmas feasts are prepared and families gather together to open gifts and eat a Christmas dinner.

Other timely events are St. Patrick's Day, Veterans Day, Memorial Day, Columbus Day, Martin Luther King Day and Presidents' Day. These events take place on specific days of the year. People gather together to celebrate these occasions. Special activities may take place at these timely occasions.

We look forward to different, timely events and occasions because these special occasions are focused on each year. We can relax on holidays and take time off in order to celebrate. Festive times add to our lives because we can enjoy celebrating each event so that our lives are more interesting when we have different events to look forward to.

Nonfiction

FIFTY-EIGHT
PAPER DOLLS

Paper dolls are popular. Little children like to clip paper dolls out of magazines and paper doll books. Barbie dolls usually have long hair and colorful clothes. Girls enjoy covering paper dolls with different outfits and plastic shoes that slip on and off dolls.

Girls can make up events that their paper dolls are in games as pretending to play hide-in-go-seek. Paper dolls can be put on plastic horses. Little girls pretend that their paper dolls are in parades. Paper dolls become playmates especially when a child has no one else to play with.

Girls may have different kinds of paper dolls. Some paper dolls may be princesses and princes who sit on a throne. Dressing paper dolls in different outfits can be fun. It takes imagination to create play time with paper dolls.

A variety of paper dolls can be displayed on shelves and in play areas. Some paper dolls are more expensive than other paper dolls. Color books may have images of different dolls that children can color in different colors to add artistic designs and colors so the dolls look good.

Paper dolls have been available for over 80 years. They are manufactured so that they can be enjoyed and used for different purposes. Children can continue to play with paper dolls.

Fiction

FIFTY-NINE
MAKING EXCUSES

Excuses are made when a person doesn't want to face up to a problem or experience which he or she doesn't want to accept. A person procrastinates when he or she becomes too busy or unable to complete a task or responsibility. Excuses may be made to cover up for lack of organization or because a person refuses to complete what is expected of him or her.

Velma Whitfield was a busy person. She had many things to do every day. Because she was so busy she put a number of things to the side to do at another time. For instance, Velma put off sewing a dress. She spent little time practicing the clarinet. She didn't complete her homework which was due the next day at school. Velma made excuses to her parents when they found out that she hadn't finished her homework.

Velma's parents were paying for her to learn to play the clarinet. Yet, she neglected to practice enough in order to play well enough. Velma's clarinet teacher, Mr. Hammond, was concerned that Velma had not practiced enough. Mr. Hammond told Velma that she would have to practice more if she was going to succeed at playing the clarinet. Velma told Mr. Hammond that she didn't have enough time to practice. He warned her that she would not be able to play in the school band if she didn't practice better in order to play the clarinet well enough. Mr. Hammond expected all members of the band to be prepared so they could play rhythmically and maintain the melody and correct tones so the school band could perform in the coming parade in the community.

Velma thought about Mr. Hammond's warning. She didn't want to be kicked out of the school band. When she came home from school she decided to devote more time practicing on her clarinet. She went over the notes carefully and tried to maintain rhythm. She tapped her foot to keep the rhythm. She went over the notes on the clarinet over and over until she could play them better.

Then the phone rang. Velma answered it. Her boyfriend, Pete had called her. Velma began talking to him. She spent nearly an hour on the phone talking to him. She finally said goodbye and hung up. It was dinner time. Velma was expected to help prepare the evening meal and to set the table. She went into the kitchen. Her mother said, "Where have you been? I expected you to help me with dinner!" Velma looked at her mother apprehensively and replied, "I have been busy practicing the clarinet." Her mother responded. "I haven't heard you practice for the last hour! What have you been doing?"

Velma didn't want to tell her mother that she was talking to Pete, her boyfriend. She made up a lie to excuse herself. She said, "I have been doing homework." Velma's mother replied, "You are supposed to do your homework after dinner. Please be on time to help me with dinner from now on." Velma began setting the dinner table. Then Velma cut some tomatoes and placed them on a plate. She put the sliced tomatoes on the dining room table. She folded napkins and placed them under each fork. There would be four family members at the table for dinner. Velma had a younger brother, Bob, as well as her parents coming to the dinner table.

After dinner Velma helped to wash the dinner dishes. Her parents had asked her how she was doing at school during dinner. Velma remarked that she was doing well. She knew she hadn't done her homework. She didn't want her parents to know that she was falling behind in school.

Velma finally went back to her bedroom once the dinner dishes were done. She sat down at a corner desk and began doing her homework. She needed to complete an assignment in Algebra. She had 40 problems to answer. She was supposed to write an essay for her English class about "Magic." She was feeling tired from her busy day. She didn't finish the essay. She hoped her English teacher would not grade her down if she turned her essay in late. She would make an excuse to her English teacher the next day about being late regarding the due assignment.

The next day Velma went to school. She brought her clarinet, her school books and a sack lunch which her mother prepared for her. Velma took the school bus to the high school. She was a junior in high school. She stepped off the school bus and walked to her English class first. The English teacher asked the students to turn in their essays. Velma knew her essay was not finished. Miss Jenkins asked Velma why she had not turned in her essay during the English class. Velma made up an excuse that her mother was ill and she had to take care of her mother. Velma pleaded with Miss Jenkins to extend her time regarding the essay. Miss Jenkins responded, "Velma, this is the third time you have been late with your assignments! You are expected to turn your homework in on time! Please have your essay ready by tomorrow!"

Velma looked at Miss Jenkins with a frown. She answered, "Yes, Miss Jenkins." Velma left the English class when the school bell rang. She went to her band class next with her clarinet. Mr. Hammond was writing something on the blackboard when the band students were arriving for the band class. All the band students sat at their assigned, band seats. Velma sat near the front near other clarinet players. Mr. Hammond explained what he had written on the chalk board. He said the band would be playing at a community festival in two weeks in a parade. He had written the time, day and place on the chalkboard. He asked the band students to write down this information. Velma and the other students wrote this information down in their notebooks.

Mr. Hammond instructed the band students to play "When The Saints Come Marching In." Velma put the music on a music stand. She positioned her clarinet to play this piece. The band began to play. Velma hit the wrong notes. Mr. Hammond, who was directing the band, said, "Stop! I hear some off key notes. Let's start over." The band began to play the melody again. Velma made the same mistakes. Mr. Hammond stopped the band again. He looked at Velma with a stern expression. He said, "Velma! You are playing the wrong notes! I told you to practice!" Velma's face turned red. She felt embarrassed. She said, "I practiced after school yesterday. I am trying to play the right notes." Mr. Hammond came over to Velma. He instructed her how to play the piece. Velma began to play the notes better.

MARVELOUS REFLECTIONS

Mr. Hammond instructed the band to play "When The Saints Come In" again. Velma played better this time. Mr. Hammond had the band play the entire piece. After band class Mr. Hammond called Velma over to him. He told her that she would have to practice the band pieces over and over in order to play the notes correctly. He warned her that she would not be allowed to play at the coming festival in two weeks if she kept making obvious mistakes. Velma said she would practice.

When Velma went home that day she became preoccupied with different things around the house. Her girlfriend, Dolores came over. They played video games and watched television. She neglected to practice her clarinet. She still hadn't completed her essay for the English class. Dolores went home at 10 p.m. that night. Velma was tired. She didn't want to stay up to do her homework.

The next day Miss Jenkins asked Velma to turn in her essay which was already overdue. Velma looked at Miss Jenkins grudgingly. She said she had not finished the essay. Miss Jenkins responded. "You were given a chance to turn it in today. Each day you are late I will lower the grade on this essay!" Velma said, "I haven't had time to do this essay." She was making excuses. She knew she had spent time playing video games and watching television with her school friend, Dolores.

Velma needed to use her time better and put first things first. Her homework should have been completed before she did other things she wanted to do. Velma needed to develop more responsibility in order to complete her school work and chores at home.

Fiction

SIXTY
MEMORIES

Positive memories are golden flashbacks which can inspire us to reflect on significant experiences we remember. Negative memories affect our feelings and attitudes. All of our memories are recorded in our akashic records. Our memories are stored in our memory bank and kept in our subconscious.

Yul Tanner had a vivid memory of his past. He could remember many experiences he had as a toddler. He remembered when he first learned to walk. He remembered when he started learning to speak. He recalled when he fell and cut his knee. It took time for his knee to heal.

Yul attended elementary and high school as well as college and graduate school. Yul earned a B.S. in Science and Ph.D. in Nuclear Science. Yul was an intelligent, well rounded person. He had a sense of humor and he had developed an understanding of human nature and behavior. He realized that his memory was important. All he had learned was recorded in his mind. Without a memory of the past, Yul would not be able to identify with his immediate family if he lost his memory of his growing up years. He relied on his memory to recall what he had learned year by year. He was able to awaken to higher consciousness and still refer to his memories in order to realize what he had already learned. He compared his memories of past experiences so he could realize how to interpret his present experiences.

Yul continued to grow and develop his awareness of many topics, issues and subjects. He was curious and inquisitive. He kept on learning all he could. He reflected on his memories. He had many valuable and worthwhile memories which he recalled. Yul learned to forgive unpleasant times in his life. He knew that if he held grudges and resentments he would be unhappy and out of balance. So, Yul learned to transmute wrongdoing and unkind deeds and negative actions. He was cleared of unnecessary fears, doubts and lower emotions. He felt free and liberated because he had control of his lower emotions. He had developed higher consciousness and enlightenment. He learned to raise his vibrations. He became One with Infinite Mind and Cosmic Reality. He maintained positive memories while he detached himself from lower unrealities and negative memories. Yul had become a God realized, fulfilled individual. His life was blissful and peaceful because of his illumined awareness.

Nonfiction

SIXTY-ONE
THE BALLET

Attending ballets can be an exciting and worthwhile experience. Ballets are performed in large theaters and opera houses on large stages. A large, spacious stage is necessary so that ballerinas have enough room to move around freely.

One of the most famous ballets is THE SWAN LAKE ballet. This ballet has been performed for many years at a lake moving about very gracefully. The SWAN LAKE is a classical ballet. It is a well known ballet around the world.

THE NUTCRACKER SUITE is another famous, well known ballet. Elves and children dance on the stage to add to the ambiance and joy of graceful movement. The magic of the nutcracker adds to the theme. Colorful costumes add to the story and décor.

Ballet is a wistful, majestic, moving experience. Ballerinas wear ballerina shoes. They lift their toes and stand on their tip toes as they dance across the stage individually and in groups. Ballerinas dance in rhythm to orchestra music. They look magnificent on the stage as they express different scenes and moods. They act out the story by dancing to express what is happening step by step in the ballet. Ballets are unique and worth attending. Ballerinas train for years to become professional ballerinas. So, go to ballets to appreciate this creative experience.

Fiction

SIXTY-TWO
INTERESTING TIMES

Interesting times make life more worthwhile. Each stimulating memory of something significant adds to the joy of living. Life is a precious opportunity to learn all we can and to enjoy wonders of nature in the world. Some manmade entertainment adds to the adventure and excitement of living day by day.

Jane Stillman was an adventurer. She enjoyed Girl Scouts while she was growing up. She went hiking, camping and boating. Jane went camping near Lake Tahoe in upper California. She packed camping equipment in a backpack such as a bedroll, cooking utensils and extra clothes and a few other personal items.

Jane went with twenty other Girl Scouts in a car up to Lake Tahoe. This lake is the longest, deepest lake in California. Jane brought several pocket knives, ropes, a small hammer and metal spikes used to pitch a tent. She was prepared to camp outdoors. It was early summer. So, it had warmed up near Lake Tahoe.

When the Girl Scouts arrived at Lake Tahoe they observed that this lake was a deep blue color. They found a place to establish a camping spot. They unpacked their camping equipment. Then they pitched enough tents on the ground close to the lake. They had to tie ropes around the stakes which were hammered into the ground to hold each tent down. Once the ten tents were set up the girl scouts put their bedrolls and camping equipment in the tents.

The next thing was to build a campfire so they could cook meat, potatoes and vegetables. The girls prepared lunch. They cooked hamburger patties to make hamburgers. They warmed up beans and cut raw vegetables such as celery, carrots and string beans to steam in a large pot with sliced potatoes. Once the food was prepared the 21 Girl Scouts sat down to eat. They viewed the beautiful, deep blue lake. They watched silver fish jump up out of the lake and dip back into the lake. There were some boats with people moving on the lake. The Girl Scouts were intrigued with the magnificent view of the lake and surrounding, evergreen forests.

After lunch the Girl Scouts cleaned up their camp. They decided to hike near the edge of the lake. They came to a boat rental dock. They decided to go boating. So, they rented four row boats. Five girls sat in each boat. They began rowing the boats with several paddles across the deep lake.

While the Girl Scouts rowed in the rowboats they were able to see many trees in the distance. They passed other boats. They went for miles in the four row boats as they paddled the boats. They were having a good time as they rowed farther and farther across Lake Tahoe. This was the first time many of the girls had a view of this lake. They took photographs of Lake Tahoe.

After rowing for ten miles the Girl Scouts decided to turn around to paddle back to their campsite. It took several hours to paddle back to their camp. It was beginning to get dark. The sun was setting. Beautiful crimson colors orange and pink emerged at the horizon. The sunset was visible. Vivid colors of red, yellow-orange and pink lit up the sky. The sunset colors reflected in the lake. The girl scouts enjoyed the splendid sunset.

When the girls returned to their campsite they tied the rowboats and anchored them near the shore. It was time to light the campfire and to cook dinner. They prepared a meat and vegetable stew in several large pots. Bread was toasted over the camp fire. Hot cider was prepared. The girls roasted popcorn for dessert. They ate their evening meal while they gazed at a bright, full moon over the lake.

After the evening meal the girls sang a variety of popular songs and folk songs as they sat around the campfire. They looked up at the stars in the night sky. The moon kept moving across the sky. The Girl Scouts went into their tents. Two girls shared each tent.

During the night sounds of owls hooting could be heard. The night air was cooler. The girls kept warm in their bedrolls inside their tents. Snakes and insects were crawling on the ground near the campsite. The girls zipped up their tents to keep wild animals, snakes and insects out of their tent.

The next morning after breakfast the Girl Scouts took the rented boats back to the rental dock. They hiked back to their campsite. They took their tents down later in the day after they went swimming in the cold, lake water. The lake water was fresh. The girls enjoyed swimming in Lake Tahoe. They stayed closer to the edge of the lake because it is very deep.

The Girl Scouts stepped back into their cars and drove back to their homes at least one hundred miles southwest. They had a wonderful time on their camp out at Lake Tahoe. They planned to go on more camping trips in the future.

Nonfiction

SIXTY-THREE
BEAUTY AND TRUTH

Beauty and truth are synonymous. We can expand our awareness and appreciation of nature. Beauty is harmonious lines, colors and forms in tune with God, the Creator of all life. Unity and oneness with all life helps us appreciate beauty everywhere.

Souls can be initiated and educated to be aware of different types of beauty. Our oneness with our I Am Presence helps us appreciate the beauty of God creations. We are able to appreciate the beauty of roses, colors in the rainbow and shapes, designs and colors of gemstones. We are able to appreciate the beauty of vivid sunrises and sunsets.

Beauty has perfect symmetry balance and equilibrium. God created us in His image. We should observe God in all living things. God intended for our Earth to be beautiful. We have majestic evergreen trees, many lakes, rivers and streams. Two-thirds of the Earth is covered with water. We have an opportunity to observe and appreciate nature. We should continue to learn about different forms of life.

We should seek truth about how life was created on Earth. How and why were trees, flowers, animals and human beings created as beautiful creations? Why has God created many forms of life on Earth? What is the truth about the evolution of life on planet, Earth? We should seek the answers about how and why life exists on Earth. Beauty is everywhere on Earth.

Nonfiction

SIXTY-FOUR
AROUND AND AROUND WE GO

Around and around we go circling and circling around a ballroom as we dance. As we circle around we twirl around our dance partner. Around we move on the dance floor in rhythm with the melodic music. We create patterns of graceful footsteps as we are dancing across the ballroom in our eloquent ballroom gowns and dress suits.

Around and around we go on a Merry Go Round on a wooden horse or other wooden object as the Merry Go Round continues to circle around. We ride side by side or in front or back of someone else. We see people watching us ride on the Merry Go Round.

Up and down and around we go on a Ferris Wheel. We see far away as we move around and around. We can ride ponies or donkeys around and around in a circle. We follow other ponies or donkeys. Ponies or donkeys are tied to a carousel. So, they naturally move in a circular direction.

Around and around we go when we run around a race track in a race. We can run around a track to exercise. We go around and around every time we run around a track.

Around and around we go when we drive into a circular parking lot or driveway. We drive around and around until we find a parking place. There are a variety of reasons why we go around and around.

Nonfiction

SIXTY-FIVE
UNDERWATER CITIES

Underwater cities may exist under the ocean. The Great Barrier Reef has a deep trench. In fact, this is the deepest trench in the world. It has been stated that extraterrestrial beings have gone to the Mariana Trench in their spacecraft

A hidden, underwater city was built by extraterrestrial beings in the ocean so they can have a place to live away from the surface of the Earth. Their dwellings are domes with connecting tunnels. The extraterrestrial beings walk through tunnels from one dome to another dome.

Another underwater city may exist near Chile in South America approximately one hundred miles in the ocean. UFOs have been seen landing in the ocean near Chile. They dive quickly into the ocean and disappear. UFOs have been seen coming out of the ocean near Chile as well. Extraterrestrial beings have established an underwater city many years ago. Extraterrestrial beings decided to build their dwellings in the ocean where they felt safe and hidden from people. They keep their spacecraft at the bottom of the ocean.

UFOs have been seen dipping down into the ocean at Catalina Island. It is possible that there is an under-water city in the ocean near Catalina Island. Extraterrestrial beings need a place to stay. They prefer to dive in the ocean in an underwater city to support their way of life.

MARVELOUS REFLECTIONS

Future generations of humanity may live under the ocean in underwater cities to survive. They will be able to live off of sea life and sea plants. They will have to produce oxygen in order to breathe inside under- water dwellings.

Fiction

SIXTY-SIX
THE TIME MACHINE

H.G. Wells wrote THE TIME MACHINE in the Nineteenth Century. He described a time machine which was used to travel into the future. The main character traveled two or three thousands years into the future. As a Nineteenth Century scientist he found out that a future generation of human beings were ignorant and dependent on a mutant group of humans who lived inside the Earth. These mutant beings were cannibals. Young women and men on the Earth's surface were victims because they were trapped underground and used for food for the mutant beings. The Nineteenth Century scientist eventually went back to his time to tell his friends and associates about the future. They didn't believe him.

If you were to travel in a time machine into time you would enter the fourth dimension. The vibration and energy increases so you can go into the fourth dimension. H.G. Wells was ahead of his time when he created the idea of a time machine which could travel into time to find out what happened to human beings in the future.

Time is relative and timelessness exists on higher planes. A time machine would disappear in the location where it began in time because this time machine would be traveling in time. Time causes changes. We live in a given time. If we reincarnate we experience embodiments in different, historical times. We learn from each embodiment. We evolve through time. Our physical bodies are our homes to house our spirits during each embodiment. We travel in time.

In between lifetimes certain souls may be able to choose the next time, place and parents of their next embodment. Some souls are more aware and alert. Therefore, they are given an opportunity to choose their future relationships.

Fiction

SIXTY-SEVEN
WANTING THINGS

Many people want material things such as expensive houses, expensive cars, valuable jewelry and many more things. People think material things are important as well as needed. They don't want to live in shacks and wear shabby clothing and cheap jewelry. They want the most expensive things they can get with money.

Melva Brooks grew up in an impoverished family in a slum area in Los Angeles, California. She worked hard from an early age because she took care of four brothers and five sisters. As the oldest child she assumed many responsibilities in her family's household. She had a few inexpensive blouses, pants, stockings, shoes, sweaters and one coat.

Melva was used to having few things. She didn't want much because she was raised with few benefits. When she attended school she saw other children wearing more expensive clothes. Girls wore beautiful ear rings, bracelets and necklaces to school. They wore attractive shoes and expensive coats and sweaters to school. Melva knew she came from a poor family. Her parents weren't able to buy her expensive clothes and things.

Melva wondered if she would be able to purchase the things other people had someday. She felt that she was deprived because she wasn't able to indulge as well as have luxurious things. She longed for the time when she could get a job in order to pay for expensive things which she wished she could have.

Melva continued to do chores around the house and to look after her brothers and sisters until she graduated from high school. She attended a few school dances. She purchased dresses at Goodwill stores which were inexpensive so she could attend school dances. Her dresses weren't as attractive as other school girls. Melva felt self conscious because she wasn't dressed as well as other school girls at the dances. Boys asked her to dance because they didn't take notice of her clothes. Melva was glad she wasn't rejected because she was poor.

After high school Melva looked for a job as a waitress. She put her applications in at several restaurants. She hoped to get a waitress position as soon as possible. Melva waited two weeks to hear from different employers. She finally accepted a position as a waitress at a nearby café entitled Comfortable Dining. She was required to purchase a uniform. Melva went to a uniform store and selected a black and white uniform.

The next Monday Melva began working at the Comfortable Dining Restaurant. She wore her new uniform. She was shown how to take food orders and how to write each order on a menu receipt pad. She began taking orders at different tables. She greeted each customer with a smile. She wrote down their orders. She brought the written orders to the cook. She brought water and drinks to the tables. She was friendly and efficient. Melva received tips because customers appreciated her service.

Weeks went by. Melva worked for six days a week. She had one day off a week. She earned minimum wages plus tips. She earned money she could save. She also gave money to her parents to help them pay their bills. Gradually Melva saved more and more money. She decided to open a checking and savings account at a nearby bank. She was able to buy some new clothes which she wore when she had a day off. Melva knew it would take years for her to save enough money to buy other things she wanted. She kept working six days a week to earn a living.

Within three years Melva decided to move away from her parents' home because she had saved enough money to rent a small apartment. She put the first and last months rent down for a one bedroom apartment in a middle class neighborhood. She moved into the one bedroom apartment. Then she began buying furniture to put in each room. The new furniture was attractive but not expensive. Melva decorated her rented apartment so she could feel comfortable and proud of how it looked.

Once Melva was settled in her apartment she was able to invite relatives and friends to come to dinner or for a visit to have snacks and beverages. She enjoyed her independence and her new lifestyle in her new neighborhood. She hoped to make new friends in this part of Los Angeles. So, she began going to social events when she had her day off. Melva attended church and a singles group. She dressed up and fixed her hair in an attractive manner so she would look attractive. She was only 24 years old. She wanted to meet eligible bachelors. Someday she might meet someone to marry.

Melva continued to pay rent each month to stay in her one bedroom apartment. She met different men at church and at dance clubs downtown Los Angeles. She began dating some of the men she became acquainted with at church. Then, one day Melva met a man by the name of Jim Matherson. He was approximately 6 feet tall with dark hair and blue eyes. Jim was handsome and well built. He was wearing tan pants, a sports shirt and sports, slip-on, matching shoes.

Melva was impressed with Jim. He behaved like a charming gentleman. He was an interesting conversationalist. Melva enjoyed listening to him speak about his interests and books he had read. He was the most interesting man she had met. So, Melva went out on dates with Jim. They went out to dinner to different, exotic restaurants. They went to museums, art galleries, parks and the L.A Zoo. They enjoyed bowling and tennis. Melva felt Jim was the right person for her.

Jim Matherson was a successful architect in Los Angeles. He had established his own private business as the head architect in a well known firm. Jim had become wealthy over a period of ten years. He was 34 years old and he had never been married.

Jim was attracted to Melva. He had fallen in love with her. Melva never revealed that she grew up in a slum area in Los Angeles. She didn't want Jim to know her past. So, she decided not to tell him how impoverished she was during her growing up years. After a period of ten months Jim proposed to Melba one day when he took her out in his expensive car. He stopped at the beach during sunset. He was in a romantic place at the beach

when he proposed to her. Melva accepted his marriage proposal joyfully. Jim was pleased that she said she would marry him. The happy couple set a date for their wedding. They decided to get married in June of that year.

Melvin was excited and happy to get married. She was 27 years old and she had never been married before. She looked forward to getting married in June. She didn't inquire about his financial status. She loved Jim for himself. Jim loved Melva for herself. She was warm and fun to be with. He genuinely loved her and cared about her.

Melva was happier than she had ever been in her life. She looked forward to a happy future. In June, Jim and Melva were married at a Unitarian Church in Los Angeles. They went on a honeymoon for several months. They traveled around Europe and enjoyed many exciting places.

When Jim and Melva returned to Los Angeles Jim took Melva to an elaborate, two story home with an enormous yard in Santa Monica, California which was not far from Los Angeles. This home was surrounded with magnificent gardens. The interior of this two story home was very eloquent and spacious with four bedrooms, a lounge room, a large living room, a spacious kitchen and dining room.

Melva had always wanted to live in such an eloquent home. Her wish had come true. Jim told Melva to buy whatever she wanted. She was able to purchase expensive clothes, furniture and jewelry because he had plenty of money in the bank. She had become wealthy, too, by being married to a wealthy husband. She was amazed at her new lifestyle in an upper class neighborhood. She had everything she wanted and more. Most of all, Melva was happy because she genuinely loved her husband, Jim.

Nonfiction

SIXTY-EIGHT
BEGINNINGS AND ENDINGS

Life is full of beginnings and endings. We begin life through birth. We end our physical life when we die. When we read a book we start at the beginning. Eventually we read the whole book and come to the end of the book. Stories, poems, essays and theses have a beginning and ending.

Stage plays, films and videos start with a beginning and finish with endings. An artist begins a painting and illustrates and works on a painting until he or she has finished the painting with ending strokes.

Swimmers begin swimming in a race. They swim back and forth across a pool until the race ends. Boatmen paddle across a lake and back until they have finished boating. A sunrise begins in the East and ends with a sunset in the West.

We begin a meal and eat until we have finished the meal. We begin to wash our teeth. We continue to brush our teeth until we have finished brushing them. Children begin to play at recess at school. When the school bell rings children must finish playing and go back to class because they are expected to finish playing to return to their classrooms.

Each day begins when the sun comes up over the horizon. The day ends when the sun goes over the horizon. The Moon comes up and eventually disappears. We look as far as we can until we see the horizon. We don't see beyond the horizon from where we are gazing. Bells begin ringing and they stop ringing and end their singing sound.

Everything has a beginning and ending on the physical plane. We wake up in the morning. Then we go to sleep at night. We need to realize beginnings and endings and to learn to accept them in our lives.

Nonfiction

SIXTY-NINE
MARVELS

There are many marvels in life. We can observe a vivid sunrise and extraordinary sunset. The bright colors of yellow, pink, red, orange, purple and magenta stand out in creative patterns across the sky.

The sparkles of dewdrops on blades of grass, leaves and in puddles are marvelous to observe in nature. Gemstones have magnificent colors and designs. Gold gleams and diamonds glitter in the light. Other gems such as opals, jade and amethysts are marvelous to observe. Pearls found in oysters are beautiful especially when they are polished.

The shape of the Alps is magnificent with high-pointed slopes covered with white snow. Glaciers are enormous and have existed for millions of years. Glaciers slide into valleys below and into the ocean. Glaciers contain a lot of ice which can slide because of loud sounds and earthquakes. Glaciers come crashing down swiftly to cover landscapes below. Glaciers that fall into the ocean cause icebergs to float like small islands. Icebergs provide places for seals, walruses and seabirds to dwell on.

Waterfalls are marvelous to observe. The multiple waterfalls at Yosemite are some of the highest waterfalls in the world. The sun reflects on some of the waterfalls at Yosemite National Park. Niagra Falls are marvelous to observe. Many rivers merge together and fall into one enormous river. Rainbows are reflected over Niagra Falls which are magnificent to witness. Angel Falls in South America are splendid to observe. There are many waterfalls around the world worth observing because they are marvelous to view.

Nonfiction

SEVENTY
MISSIONARY SERVICE

Missionary service has been taking place for hundreds of years. Christian missionaries began with the Catholic Church over 500 years ago. Catholic priests and monks traveled from Spain and Portugal to America. They traveled by ships to the California coast.

Father Serra was the first priest to bring other Catholic monks as Christian missionaries with him to California. Father Serra built 21 Catholic missions from San Diego to upper California. Most of the Catholic missions were built along the California coast.

The purpose of the Catholic missions was to introduce Christianity to the American Indians and to settlers who came to California to live. The Catholic missionaries spread Christianity. They taught the Golden Rule and about brotherhood, charity and service to others. They focused on the teachings of Jesus Christ. Christianity spread in America.

Other Christian churches have Christian missionaries such as the Seventh Day Adventists, the Lutherans and Jehovah Witnesses. These Christian missionaries travel around the world to spread Christianity to different countries. They live among people in villages, towns and cities to convert followers into Christians.

Christianity is one of the most well known religions in the world today. Millions of people have become Christians. Christian knights defended Christianity when Europeans were invaded by Moslems in the 13th and 14th centuries. They established churches around Europe. The knights during the Christian Crusades fought to protect Christianity.

Christian missionaries continue to spread the teachings of Jesus Christ around the world. They teach others that our true salvation is to be saved by Jesus Christ, our Lord, who is the King of Kings.

Nonfiction

SEVENTY-ONE
THE PEACE CORPS YESTERDAY AND TODAY

The Peace Corps was established by John F. Kennedy, one of our American presidents. He established the Peace Corps in the early 1960s. The purpose of the Peace Corps was to send Peace Corps workers to underprivileged countries to serve as helpers to the needy people in different cultures who needed assistance in learning how to improve farming techniques and to improve sanitation and other living conditions.

Underprivileged people need to learn to take care of themselves by improving their living standards. They need to cultivate soil and plant seeds to create enough food to eat. These people need to learn to maintain much better sanitation standards. Plumbing needs to be improved in slum areas.

Peace Corps workers teach underprivileged people to eat healthy food such as raw, organic fruits and vegetables. Underprivileged people need to have fresh, safe, clean water to drink. Clothes need to be washed regularly to wear. These people need to bathe regularly to maintain better health. Peace Corps workers teach underprivileged people to build sturdy houses which are more comfortable to live in

The purpose today is for the Peace Corps to continue to serve needy, underprivileged people around the world. The use of modern appliances and agricultural equipment is being used to improve

MARVELOUS REFLECTIONS

living conditions in deprived regions of the world. More and more needy people are learning to become self sufficient and are more capable of living better lives. When living conditions are improved people have more hope and faith in living better lives.

Nonfiction

SEVENTY-TWO
RANDOM OCCURRENCES

Random occurrences take place from time to time. People take risks when they go to casinos to gamble. They may gamble away a lot of money before they win a small amount of money. Few people win a lot of money at casinos. There is a random chance that a person is able to win a sum of money. This is why gamblers may go broke because they may seldom win.

When dice are thrown on the table random chance occurs because the dice may not tumble the way the dice thrower hopes they will fall. Dice are thrown frequently. Yet, few dice throwers succeed in receiving the winning score. Random chance occurs which may alter who will win or who will not win. No one is absolutely sure who will be the winner. It is a risk to gamble anytime because you can't be sure of the outcome. Most likely you will lose money.

When a roulette wheel is used in a gambling hall people bet on a certain number or letter. If their number isn't selected they automatically lose. Their number is one of many random numbers. So, they may have a slight chance of winning.

Random occurrences exist when people play bingo. Certain numbers are called. Specific numbers are on bingo cards. It is random chance if enough numbers are called which are on players' bingo cards. One person will win out of the entire group of bingo players.

MARVELOUS REFLECTIONS

Random occurrences exist when individuals play cards. They may be dealt a good hand or a bad group of cards. If a person receives a bad group of cards he or she will not be able to win a game. It is by random selections that cards are passed out to card players. Players must receive the cards randomly. Once all the cards are dealt out each player looks at their cards. The game is won by players who receive the most points or the best cards.

One person out of hundreds of people may win a sum of money. This winner may be selected randomly. Prize winners may be selected randomly. Random occurrences may take place for many reasons.

Nonfiction

SEVENTY-THREE
EXTINCTION OF DINOSAURS

Dinosaurs were known to live over 65 million years ago. Many types of enormous reptiles roamed the Earth for thousands of years. There was plenty of water and vegetation. So, the dinosaurs thrived around the world.

The scientists and archaeologists have theorized in the twentieth century that dinosaurs were destroyed approximately 65 million years ago. Many of the dinosaurs became extinct on major continents because a large asteroid fell to Earth. Dust storms destroyed the atmosphere. Water disappeared and the Earth's surface cracked open. Dinosaurs died by the thousands.

However, recent evidence has been revealed which indicates that ancient people in Mexico have made drawings in caves and rocks of dinosaurs which they saw while they were living on Earth. This means that some dinosaurs survived the cataclysm millions of years ago. The dust storms may not have covered the entire face of the whole Earth. Therefore, some dinosaurs may have continued to live on the Earth's surface.

The blue gila monster is a large reptile which lives on a Polynesian island known as The Galapagos Islands. This large reptile has lived on these islands for thousands of years.

In Scotland, a giant, long necked serpent has been seen in Loch Ness Lake. It appears to come form ancient times. Giant turtles may have lived during the dinosaur age. Dinosaurs in general are extinct today.

Nonfiction

SEVENTY-FOUR
BROTHERHOOD AND SISTERHOOD

Brotherhood is when someone practices the Golden Rule. The Golden Rule means that we should treat someone else as blood kin. We should do unto others as we would like to be treated. Sisterhood means the same as brotherhood.

Whenever we are kind, loving and thoughtful we are practicing brotherhood and sisterhood. Every thought, word and deed is important. What we do for others in a worthwhile way brings us positive karma known as cause and effect.

Right action and consideration benefits others as well as ourself. Every good deed reaps positive responses. Positive karma takes place when we earn it.

Jesus Christ practiced the Golden Rule. He practiced brotherhood in his daily life. Some people recognized him as the Christ. It took some time for changes to be made so that Christianity could spread around the world. Jesus Christ set an example in his life consistently. He was a gentle, kind person who served humanity. He healed sick and afflicted souls while he was living on Earth.

Because Jesus Christ practiced brotherhood he also went to his ascension after he was crucified on the cross. Sisterhood is practiced by women. More women are demonstrating sisterhood. Service and goodwill are practiced in the world. Women and men, who become effective leaders, help to make positive changes in the world. These individuals practice brotherhood and sisterhood. We all have the opportunity to practice the Golden rule by demonstrating brotherhood and sisterhood.

Nonfiction

SEVENTY-FIVE
EXPLORATIONS AND SETTLEMENTS

Explorations have taken place over millions of years. Many explorers have traveled from one continent to another continent. Navigators have traveled by boats and ships across different oceans in order to reach other places. Once explorers discovered new landscapes they established new settlements in many places.

Early America was explored by English, French, Spanish and Dutch explorers. Thirteen English colonies were established along the upper east Coast of North America. Settlers traveled West through central landscapes to the West Coast which was thousands of miles away.

During ancient times tribesmen migrated from Asia to Alaska, Canada and other lands in America. These Asiatic peoples settled in North America. They became Canadian and American tribes who settled new landscapes. The North American Indians lived in the new lands for thousands of years. Europeans fought against American Indians and took over most of the land. American Indians were forced into Indian reservations in less desirable land.

Polynesian people traveled in large canoes across the ocean to other South Sea islands. Many South Sea islands were populated by Polynesian peoples. In time, Europeans have explored many South Sea islands through the years. Europeans have settled in the Hawaiian Islands, Thomas Islands, Philippine Islands, Samoa,

Tahiti, Australia, New Zealand and Micronesian Islands, etc. in the Pacific Ocean.

Exploration and settlement of new lands by explorers and settlers has made a big difference in the development of many continents in the world. The planet, Earth has approximately 6 billion people today.